Life With Grandma and Grandpa
After Prison

Ken Halverson

authorHOUSE®

AuthorHouse™
1663 Liberty Drive, Suite 200
Bloomington, IN 47403
www.authorhouse.com
Phone: 1-800-839-8640

First published by AuthorHouse 4/7/2009

ISBN: 978-1-4389-3236-1 (sc)

Printed in the United States of America
Bloomington, Indiana

This book is printed on acid-free paper.

Contents

Forward

After I wrote "If Grandma's in Heaven, Watch Out", a lot of readers wanted to know what happened to everyone. I'll refresh the night they were caught and take you into the prison where they each ended up.

People also asked me what I did for work before I retired. I was a Park Ranger for a large city just north of Minneapolis. I was also a Reserve Police Officer for that city and rose to the rank of Sergeant. I had on-going training for my Park Ranger position through the Police Reserve program. Prior to being a Park Ranger I drove a motor coach across the country. It was another great job. I saw most of the USA and several states many times.

This book goes deeper into my Grandparents life after prison. They were both hardened by the 1930's depression and prison confinement. They would take out their anger on each other and their family.

Duco could have been saved from his criminal activities if it wasn't for Mable. He would have strolled into obscurity and been a better person. His weakness for beer and sex is what put him in the arms of Mable. Mable would have stayed the course. Her life of crime was molded from her influential brothers and the fact that she left home at a very young age. Some say the economic depression drove people like her to crime. I disagree with that. Crime is a choice, not a social accepted excuse to hurt others because of hard times. Some say it happened long ago and it's time to forgive and forget. No way, it's a part of history. I believe the only ones that can forgive them should be the victims and their God.

The 63 crimes they confessed to in 1933 were all felonies. Thinking back about the confessions, I wonder how many crimes they didn't confess to. They got away with 61 of them. The men were convicted on the 1st degree robbery at Coggins and the women were convicted of kidnapping Mr. Clay Johnson. They tried to kill a police officer that night and got away with it. They also held up several other stores prior to Coggins and got away with it. No doubt, they got off easy. They would never be prosecuted for any more crimes. If they were to be prosecuted for other felonies the committed in Minneapolis, they would have went to prison for life.

The gang had to know this. I never found any plea bargaining that would let them off the hook for the other crimes. I just can't understand why they were not prosecuted further. I understand that Swift County didn't have a lot of money available for more prosecution but these trials could have been conducted in Hennepin County, Minnesota. That county wasn't strapped for funds to put them on trial.

Personally, I believe they should have spent a minimum of 20 years without parole, the women too. Maybe that would have cooled their heels. The men spent about 7 years. Think about how they tried to kill a police officer while performing a felony robbery. That should have been a heavier sentence. There is no way a person could get away this today. Our police officers are the only line of defense we have against crimes like this.

The questions I have not found an answer too is why didn't the Hennepin County Attorney press charges against the gang? They had signed confessions listing the crimes committed in Minneapolis. It's maybe too late for answers. Now the prosecutors are all gone. I don't believe there was a deal, I think Minneapolis still tolerated and harbored criminals. They could have figured that 5 to 40 years was enough punishment. Point is they didn't finish a majority of the 40 years. They were released after about 7 years. Totally free men with all their rights restored. It's no wonder that people that have been victims of a crime don't trust the judicial system. It seems to favor the rights of the prisoner and ignore the rights of the victim. I just don't believe those innocent victims were satisfied by the sentence the gangsters received from judge Qvale. Today I wonder how Mr. Clay Johnson felt about the sentences handed down. He was an attorney with criminal defense experience. Maybe this was a taste of his medicine.

Mable's two girls should have become wards of the court. Mavis was staying with her aunt Manda. I remember Manda and her husband Clarence. Mavis would have had a good home with them. Darlos was not as fortunate. The judge asked Mable where the girls should be placed. What a lame brain idea. Ask the fox where to keep the chickens. I believe Judge Qvale made the worse decision of his career. He should have at the very least talked to the girls' one on one. The court also has investigators, why didn't they investigate the girls living conditions and interview the people they were staying with? Besides not prosecuting the gang for other major felonies and not checking the girls living conditions I believe this was a judicial failure in the highest degree. With the exception of Darlos, everyone got off easy. My mother would suffer the physical and emotional problems for the rest of her life. She is the only one that received a life sentence.

So now I ask myself how did the people that had been violated by the gang on just that one night in February feel when they were completely ignored by our system. These people didn't receive justice.

1. Henry Larson first to be kidnapped after the shootout. Ed Wayne second to be kidnapped after Henry's car got stuck. Ed also had to endure a shootout with the Chippewa County Sheriff and his posse during the capture process.
2. Arnie Strand the Coggins attendant that was terrorized by the gang twice. His life was seriously threatened twice within two weeks. The gang was prosecuted on 1st degree robbery of Coggins. Not for threatening Arnie's life.
3. Benson Police Chief Oscar Johnson was the hero of the night but endured life threatening conditions with the gang firing three separate sorties of gunfire. The gang wanted him dead.

The only person that received any kind justice at all was Clay Johnson. He was the rich and famous attorney kidnapped by the gang that night. Do you think his status had anything to do with him being the only satisfied victim? When the Minneapolis Police were notified about his kidnapping from the law firm Clay Johnson was a partner in, they reacted as if a president was captured. They notified many other police departments to be on the look out for his new Buick. They perked up and took this kidnapping serious. Prior to this kidnapping, they never took others as serious.

They were tagged "The Snatchers" by police. They just never put a lot of effort into capturing them. Why not?

Since writing the first book I received hundreds of calls and met hundreds of people that enlightened me on new information and corrected information. This book is written with all the new information I have to the date of publication.

The Bonrud Gang,
1. Perley (Duco, Duke) Oliva was my step grandfather.
2. Mable (Bonrud) Oliva was my grandmother.
3. Cleon Bonrud was my great uncle.
4. Blanch Bonrud was Cleon's short timed wife. Maiden name unknown.
5. Noble Bonrud was my great uncle and the youngest Bonrud.
6. Margaret was Noble's widow. There are no photos of Margaret that I could find. Maiden name unknown.
7. Walter Christenson was Cleon's friend. They met while they were serving time in the St. Cloud, Minnesota prison. Cleon was convicted of larceny and Walter was convicted of theft.

As I grew up I was only familiar with Duco, Mable and Cleon. As far as I know the rest of the gang just went about their lives without contact with these three. Of course parole terms would have stated that they refrain from contact with known criminals and their activities, but since when did any of these people obey the rules. I just find it hard to believe that larceny left their hearts for good. They were just too hard core to go straight.

The Crime

You would think that being in prison would humanize a person and grant them a bit of humility. If the committed person had a chip on their shoulder you would think it would have been knocked off. Wasn't prison supposed to cleanse the spirit and flush away the evil that resides within the prisoner? Wasn't prison supposed to teach a profession that would enrich the life of the prisoner upon their release? If any of this is true, what the hell happened to grandma and grandpa?

In April of 1933 grandma, Mable, was convicted of kidnapping and sentenced to one year in the Shakopee Women's Reformatory. Grandpa, aka Perley, Duke or Duco, was convicted of 1st degree armed robbery and sentenced to 5-40 years of hard labor in the Stillwater State Prison. They belonged to the ruthless and dangerous Bonrud Gang that committed over 63 felony crimes in Minnesota, South Dakota and Iowa. The seven member gang met their demise in a little western Minnesota town called Benson.

After a three day drinking binge the gang kidnapped a very important attorney, Clay Johnson, and took him and his car on a crime spree stretching west along Minnesota highway 12 west from Minneapolis. The seven member gang held up several stores and gas stations along the route. Their destination was originally going to be Watertown, South Dakota, and eventually Montevideo, Minnesota, aka Monte, where they had friends and relatives and hide outs.

These were tough times in the out-lining towns and farming communities. They were suffering through the depression. Big time money people in high places caused the national financial depression and these little towns suffered because of them. A similar situation would be repeated in 2008 and 2009.

Some people took a misguided approach and became sympathizers for the gangs that robbed the rich. These were the people that the Bonrud Gang would snuggle up too and take advantage of their hospitality. As the old saying goes, "Rob the rich and share with the poor". Give money to the poor? Ha! The gang kept it. The poor can get their own. In fact, some of the poor were robbed themselves by the gang. This gang wasn't Robin Hood and his merry band of thieves.

On the night of February 26, 1933 and after a three day drinking spree the gang kidnapped and commandeered Clay Johnson and his new Buick.

Once Clay Johnson was secured to the rear seat foot rail the 7 member gang began their crime spree along Minnesota highway 10, now highway 12, in Cokato, Minnesota.

Then they hit Atwater and Litchfield, Minnesota without any problems. Continuing west on highway 10 they were getting more and more emboldened by swilling down alcohol as fast as the back seat passengers could open the bottles.

As drunk as they all were, they successfully robbed a store in Willmar, Minnesota. It was the Willmar police that figured out the gang's direction out of town and estimated that Benson was the next town they would hit.

The Willmar police notified Benson Police Chief Oscar Johnson of the danger heading his way. This was about 6:30 PM and Oscar figured that the only place open on that mild night would be Coggins Oil Station. It was on the eastern side of town and on highway 10. Oscar jumped in his squad car and went there.

Once there he hid his car in the back of the station and walked in and met up with the attendant Arnie Strand. The situation was explained to Arnie and he was requested to act normal while Oscar took up a defensive position. Arnie had a hard time acting normal. He was just robbed at gun point two weeks ago. One of the gangsters took exception to a muffled statement Arnie made and almost shot him.

In the mean time Oscar told Arnie to call his evening patrol partner Carl Tengvall who was on his supper break at the Rangaard Café. Tell him of the possible danger heading towards town and to stay there in case the gang tries to hold up the café.

About a half an hour later the car with the gangsters drove up to the front door at Coggins station. By now Oscar was crouching behind some oil barrels near the front door. Two of the gangsters jumped out of the car and dashed into the store.

Arnie panicked and was starting out the front door until he bumped into the gangsters. With their pistols drawn and pointed at Arnie, he was ordered back into the store and to the cash register. One of the gang members asked Arnie, "Did you get a gun yet?" Arnie just about fainted. These were the same men that held him up two weeks ago.

At that time Arnie muttered under his breath, "If I had a gun I'd shoot both of you." The gunman heard him and pointed his gun

3

directly between Arnie's eyes and asked him to repeat what he said a little louder. Arnie did the best thing and just closed his eyes and shut up. That probably saved his life.

Mean-while outside, Oscar was crouching and creeping towards the car to arrest the driver and then use the car for cover. As he crawled up to the car he popped up and pointed his gun inside the car and noticed five more people crouched down in the car. He recoiled backwards muttering a few unmentionables and fired off a couple shots not hitting anyone.

Hearing the shots, a split second later Walter came out of the store firing wildly in every direction except where Oscar was. Oscar fired once at him and hit Walter in the leg spinning his around. The gangster had enough momentum to get into the front seat of the car. Cleon was in the front seat and pulled Walter into the car the rest of the way. One of the women shouted out, "My God Walter, your hurt!" Noble strolled out of the store stalking and looking for a target to shoot at. As he was looking for a target, Oscar was taking close aim at Noble. Oscar fired once. Noble fell into a heap on the sidewalk. The bullet pierced his jugular vein and spinal cord. Noble never knew what hit him. He was dead when he hit the ground. The driver of the car, Duco, panicked and floored the gas pedal and sped out of the parking lot back onto highway 10 westward towards town.

They just went down the road a block or two out of gun range and stopped. Then they turned the car around facing east and stopped again. They discussed the possibility that Noble was still alive and they should rescue him. They hesitated for a minute gathering courage and then floored the new powerful Buick towards the station with all guns blazing at anything that could hide the lawman. By now Oscar moved across the street behind a tree and fired at the car from there. The gangsters heard the bullets hit the car and were confused by

4

where they came from. They again sped away going east and stopped at the stockyards a block away. Oscar said the night was so still that he heard one of the gunmen say, "Give me some shells, I'll get him yet."

Now the gang was determined to kill Oscar. In their drunken state of mind they were invincible and very pissed off. The car started another charge towards the station again with the gangsters again firing at everything that could hide a man. How drunk were these guys? Oscar was still across the street! Again Oscar opened fire hitting the car several more times. Again the gang heard the bullets striking the car. Now they thought enough is enough; one of these bullets will eventually hit one of us. They sped out of the gas station again and went west on highway 10. This time they were gone for good. The car kept going towards Benson.

I'm sure the gangsters had enough of being shot at. They thought they were in the clear until they came up to Rangaards Café. There was Carl crouched down on the shoulder of the road firing his pistol at the gang as they sped by. He hit a tire and the trunk of the car.

It should be mentioned that most police officers were issued .38 caliber revolvers as duty weapons back then. The cars back then had a heavier gauge sheet metal on the car exterior. It's no surprise that the .38's didn't pierce the car far enough into the interior to harm anyone. The bullet would have lost its velocity when it first hit the metal. It would have only been through the glass that a bullet could strike a passenger. In this case the gang was very lucky not to have been hit. They had the side windows down as they fired at Oscar. The windshield and rear windows were never hit.

In the case of the Bonnie and Clyde capture, you may have seen photos of their car after the posse ambushed them on a dirt road in the Louisiana back country. Bullets went through the doors with apparent ease. The two occupants were nearly torn into pieces from the bullets. After the bullets went through the sheet metal they would have expanded to look like a mushroom. This caused extreme trauma to the occupants. In that case rifles were used to shoot the two criminals. Two of the lawmen had BAR's, Browning Automatic Rifles. These were the most powerful guns at the time. The bullets not only penetrated the car, it went through the human target and out the other side of the car. It's been said that the bullet from a BAR could split an engine block.

The gang had enough of this town! They now wanted to get to Montevideo in a hurry. They were so shook up and panicked they missed the Highway 29 turn to Montevideo. They were just about in the town of Clontarf. They thought it would be best to stay away from any town for now. There could be more police lying in ambush just itching to take a few shots at them.

They turned off the main road onto a dirt road. Duke was driving and he said that the car was uncontrollable. He pulled off the road across the ditch and behind some trees and then stopped. They all piled out of the car and gave it an inspection. Sure enough, it had two flat tires and one spare tire. Three of them volunteered to commandeer a car, Cleon, Walter and Margaret.

It took three of them a lot of walking in the dark to finally get to a farm. The gangsters banged on the door. It was nearly 10:00 PM and Henry Larson answered the door. They told Henry that their car was broke down and they offered Henry cash if he would drive the gang to Clontarf for help.

The gang figured Henry's car would be recognized and wouldn't draw any suspicion. Henry could use the extra cash so he agreed to drive them to town. On the way to town the gangsters told him they would like to pick up the rest of the party and bring them along. Henry agreed. After they piled into Henry's car he asked for directions to the broken down car. Cleon and Walter looked at each other and scratched their heads. They were lost.

Cleon made arbitrary directions hopes he would recognize something that would help him find the way. After driving aimlessly for a short time they noticed something alright, a sign saying, "Entering Benson". "TURN THIS CAR AROUND NOW!" one of the gangsters shouted. This isn't the town they had in mind. The shocked Henry slammed on the brakes and then spun the car around.

Now one of the boys pulled out a gun and stuck it in Henry's ribs and explained what had happened. He also said the plan is to find his comrades and then take his car. Now step on it and take the next right hand turn. Henry said, "The next right is Lake Hassel Road and it is very muddy and they could get stuck." The gunman sitting next to him, Cleon, shoved his gun in Henry's face and said, "That would be very bad for you."

Henry followed orders and turned right onto Lake Hassel road. Sure enough, the car got stuck. Henry burst out, "Look, I've had enough of you boys, and I won't go any farther with you!"

Cleon reached over and opened Henry's door and pushed him out. Henry landed flat on his back in the mud. The gangster slid out and stood over Henry and with a death look he pointed his pistol at Henry's eye and pulled back the hammer of his pistol. Henry thought that this was it for him and silently said a prayer. After a few tense seconds the gunman told him to get up. He grabbed Henry by the collar to help him up. "Look you old fool. You want to die out here? If not, you will walk with me back to that farm a quarter mile back and tell them anything to get us another car.

If you don't want to do that, I'll shoot you here and you can die in the mud." Henry knew he meant business so he agreed. He knew the people that lived there.

Once they reached the farm, Henry knocked politely on the door. A minute later a sleepy eyed Ed Wayne opened the door with a look of concern. What's wrong Henry? One of the gunmen pointed a gun into Ed's face and told him to get ready for a road trip. Without a thought, Ed grabbed his car keys and led the way to the car. Henry was told to stay behind.

He was no longer needed. Once everyone was in Ed's car the gunmen explained the situation. They wanted to find their comrades and then get to Montevideo. Ed said he would help them if they didn't hurt him.

They drove around and eventually found everyone and they all climbed in the car. They were all together again except for Nobel. They all left for Montevideo and left behind their hostage and the dog. The hostage they had tied up in the shot up Buick broke himself free and started walking towards the bright lights of Benson. After a half hour and hiding from every car that sped by him he came upon the Viking Hotel.

The clerk was most accommodating. He prepared hot coffee and rolls for the beat up traveler. He was given a phone. The first call he made was to the Benson police to tell them the gang was going to Montevideo.

The Police in Benson, Oscar Johnson, called the Chippewa County Sheriff, Nells Peterson. They told Nells about the shootout and the two kidnappings. The Chippewa County Sheriff is located in Montevideo. Oscar told Nell's that credible information from the kidnapped victim would place the gang south bound on highway 29 towards Montevideo. Oscar stated he had a squad heading that way.

The Sheriff thanked Oscar for the info and hung up and then dialed up a two man posse.

Once the Sheriff had his posse together they piled into the Sheriffs' squad and headed north towards Benson. The posse was heavily armed and ready to take on a gang that had the stones to shoot at police. How dare they?

At the same time Ed was complaining to the gang that taking back roads to Montevideo was becoming treacherous. He was worried the soft road would eventually get them stuck. They gang already had one car stuck on them and they were in no mood to push a car out of the mud. The gangsters said to get on the hard top road and floor the car towards Montevideo. It was a relief to Ed. He only went a block or so to highway 29 and headed south as fast as the car would go.

A short time later the two cars passed each other on highway 29. The Sheriff could only assume the car that went by him was the gang. He slammed on the brakes and turned the car around and sped towards the gang. It didn't take the powerful squad car long to catch up to the gangsters.

The Sheriff warned his posse to use extreme caution shooting at the vehicle; after all, the driver is an innocent victim. The Sheriff caught up to the vehicle and ordered his men to fire. Salvos of several shots were fired at the car.

There was wild random return fire. Once again he ordered the posse to fire. By now the Sheriff was next to the car and he noticed the women in the car were waving white handkerchiefs and mouthing, "We surrender!" The two cars simultaneously pulled off the road onto the shoulder.

The Sheriff was about 15 feet behind the bandits. The Sheriff and posse exited their car with guns trained on the gangsters. At this time a Benson Police car also arrived on the scene and joined the Sheriff.

The Sheriff barked out, "Out of the car with hands up!" The gang was a bit slow to react. The Sheriff not taking any chances of them testing his authority fired a couple shots into the air. Again he ordered them out. The gang knew they couldn't take on 4 professional law men; they slowly exited the car with their hands up. They all lay on the ground spread eagled. The posse frisked them all and had just enough hand cuffs to subdue them.

There was an old magazine transcript that stated the gang jumped out of the car and ran into a muddy cornfield and got stuck up to their knees. I'm not so sure about this version. There were no police reports stating this. I believe they gave up after the salvo of rifle fire from the Sheriff's car. They may have sobered up enough by now to know running through a muddy field is extremely hard to do and their backs would have been exposed to gunfire. I think they gave up sitting in the car like official reports state.

The gang was now under control and under arrest. It was decided that the gang would be held in the Montevideo jail. Benson didn't have enough room and the security level was not as good as the Montevideo jail. The night of terror on the great plains of south western Minnesota was over. Or was it?

Coroner's Inquest

February 28, 1933, the Swift county Coroner, Julius Hoiland, conducted an inquest into the death of Noble Bonrud. The panel of 6 jurors was to hear testimony from anyone involved in the shooting death of Noble. Also in attendance was Joe Bonrud. Joe was the oldest in the Bonrud family of 12 children. He was there to identify his baby brother's body and after the inquest he would take the body to Baxter, Minnesota for preparation for a funeral. The coroner verified his name and purpose for being there. The coroner asked Joe if the body on the table before him was his brother Noble Bonrud. Joe stated that the body was his brother. He was never asked anymore questions. Joe had to sit alone and listen to the whole inquest with its witnesses. The coroner stated for the record that the body lying on the table before the jury was in fact identified by a sibling and the dead body is Noble Bonrud. He died from a gunshot wound that entered his neck on the right side and exited on the left. He died from immediate and terminal trauma with blood loss to the brain.

The first to testify was the original kidnapped victim Clay Johnson. He was asked how his kidnapping came about and how he was treated. Surprisingly he stated that the gang treated him quite well. This is contrary to what he reported to his law firm and Minneapolis police investigators. To them he reported the gang tied him to the back seat floor rail. When the gang departed Minneapolis to embark on the crime spree he noticed that they were already very intoxicated. The three women and one man were in the back seat opening beer bottles and spraying him with every opening. He mentioned that he was soaked in beer. The woman were all bubbly and giddy and would stomp their feet on him when they broke out in laughter. They were also playing with his dog and when the dog performed a trick they would giggle and stomp on him. During one of the armed robberies he was warned not to say anything or move. He was told that he would be shot. When the gang held up the store and gas stations all the back seat passengers would crouch down on top of him. They did this to give the impression there were only three people in the car. The man in the back seat crouched over Johnson stuck his gun in his ribs showing that he meant business. Johnson couldn't say anything. The weight of the people on top of his was making it hard to breathe much less talk. This procedure was repeated during every robbery.

His testimony to the coroner included the fact that after every robbery the gang would again open beer for everyone and would even pass a bottle of liquor. He said they were becoming extremely intoxicated and more brazen at each hold up.

Ed Wayne and Henry Larson weren't needed for testimony. Their kidnappings happened after the shooting.

The main testimony came from Police Chief Oscar Johnson. Chief Johnson was the officer that shot and killed Noble Bonrud. His testimony was calm and professional. Common questions were asked about his actions that night. He mentioned a few important facts that would make the shooting justified.

Oscar's testimony started with the warning from the Willmar police that the gang was very intoxicated and with every robbery they were becoming more threatening and dangerous. It was not stated that there could be several people in the car. The car was a new, blue in color and had the unique feature of having two tail lights. This warning set the tone for Oscar. If he should encounter this gang it may be difficult to arrest them. Benson was a small town and at the present time there are just two cars patrolling the town.

Oscar testified that the gang did show up at Coggins Station. At first the car drove slowly past the station and that's when he noticed the two tail lights. Then the car turned around and came back to the station and parked in front of the door. Oscar noticed only three men in the car and two of them just jumped out and entered the store. He went on to state that he approached the car at a near crawl to subdue the driver and then use the car as cover.

As he popped up and pointed his gun at the driver he noticed several more people crouched down in the back seat. He recoiled backwards and fired two rounds into the car harmlessly. He said that the shots alerted the holdup men and almost instantly one of them ran out the door shooting his gun wildly everywhere.

Oscar took one shot at him and hit the gangster in the upper leg. The gangster had enough momentum to get into the cars back seat. He stated that the second gunman was more cautious exiting the store. He took a few seconds to find a target to shoot at.

Oscar said he fired at him and the bullet hit the man in the neck. He fell into a heap and died nearly instantly. As he shot that man the car sped off towards town.

The testimony continued with Oscar describing the gangs' next two charges at him trying to shoot him. He said at every charge he located himself at a different place and fired at the vehicle. He said that it obviously confused the gang and after the second charge they sped off and didn't return.

Oscar said he fired 9 bullets at the gangsters. He lost count how many shots were taken at him. He did state that the night was so still, when the gang stopped at the stock yards a block away he heard the gun man say, "give me more shells, I'll get him yet". Oscar said his life was in grave danger.

Arnie Strand was he next to testify. He backed up all the testimony that the Chief of Police gave. His only difference was that when the gunmen entered the store they put their guns into his back and told him not to turn around. Then one of the gun men asked him if he ever got the gun that he wanted to shoot him with. Arnie about fainted. These two men robbed him two weeks earlier. At that time under his breath Arnie said, "If I had a gun I'd shoot you". The gun man heard that and asked him to repeat what he just said. Arnie said he closed his eyes and wouldn't say anything. He thought he would be shot then and there.

The coroner interrupted and asked Arnie, "Are you saying these gunmen robbed you before?" Arnie told them again that it happened two weeks earlier. Arnie went on to say that he heard the gun shots outside. The two robbers perked up and went for the door. He went on to state that he saw the first robber get shot in the leg and a few seconds later he saw the second gunman get shot in the neck and drop to the ground. Then the car sped off. He said the car charged the station two more times and never could find Oscars' location. He was asked if he noticed how many people in the car were shooting.

Arnie said he really couldn't tell. He saw gun flashes from the whole vehicle. This ended his testimony.

The inquest jury came to a unanimous decision that the Police Chief Oscar Johnson took appropriate actions in shooting Noble Bonrud dead. It was in the line of duty while trying to arrest robbery suspects. The jury panel was dismissed and the coroner released the body to the custody of Joe Bonrud. Joe took the body to Baxter and left it with the mortician for preparation.

A few days later the church in Baxter would conduct a funeral for Noble. At the time for the funeral the minister stood at the door and greeted everyone that entered the church. Being a small town church he knew just about everyone that attended.

The hearse arrived a short time later and parked in front of the church. The poll bearers went to the back of the hearse and pulled the casket out. In unison they marched up the sidewalk to the church.

As they approached the door the minister stood in front of the entrance and told the poll bearers to put the casket down on the sidewalk. He refused to allow the dead body of a sinner in his church. It would remain outside and unguarded during the service. The only thing that was good about this unusual action was the time of the year. It was winter and cold outside and the sun wouldn't beat so hard on the dead body in the casket.

During the service the minister theme was, "The wages of sin is death". He denounced the gang for their activities and blamed Noble's death onto himself. He deserved to die for the sins he committed. Then the minister started on the Bonrud family. They should have rescued their kin from the life of crime. It was a family affair back then and the failure of these gangsters would be blamed on the family. Why didn't the family interfere and preach Gods word into them until the devil left their spirit? The minister went on and on with his lecture.

I can't imagine how it felt to be a Bonrud during this lecture. They were being blamed for the actions of others. They thought it was totally unfair but being God fearing people they hung on every word the minister said. They figured if the minister interpreted the bible and Gods word this way, then it must be so. At the end of the service they said, "Amen". Feeling real bad about themselves they hung their heads low as they walked outside past the casket and to the side of the church to the grave site. They circled the grave and waited for the casket and the minister.

As the casket was put onto the grave stand Mable appeared with a troop of guards at her side. She was handcuffed and ankle shackled. As she approached the grave she noticed her two daughters, Mavis and Darlos, and then screamed out, "My babies, oh my babies!"

The two girls yelled out for their mother and a commotion began to stir in the crowd of over a hundred people. The guards picked up Mable and rushed her back to the squad car and sped off back to Montevideo. It took people a few minutes to settle the two girls aged 12 and 6.

Once things settled down the minister again went on about the sins of the gangster lying before them. The minister read a few bible passages and then walked away. The funeral was over. The end result of the ministers preaching's was about to begin.

As the next few days went on the Bonrud's and persons married to Bonrud's were starting to receive notices. They were informed that they were not welcome into their church of choice nor could they attend church social functions. They were no longer welcome to city functions and banned from city parks.

A lot of café's would not serve them. Some Bonrud's were even fired from their jobs. The family was being socially scorned. Most of the family lived on farms and couldn't just sell and move away. They had to band together and weather out this punishment. It would take a few years before the banishments would fade away.

The truth of the matter is that when the gang was in their prime some of the Bonrud family became sympathizers to the cause of the gang. Rob the rich people. After all, the rich were the ones that caused the depression and they should suffer some sort of punishment. The gang would do the dirty work and knock off a rich slob. The family sympathizers would listen with satisfaction to all the stories the gang would tell when they came to Montevideo.

Only one thing wrong with these stories, they were lies. Rob the rich? They robbed the poor more than the rich. They were easier to find, everyone was poor in the 1930's. Not many rich people around during a depression. So in retrospect, the minister directed a sermon to the right people, but he also delivered it to the innocent ones as well.

As evidence that there were family sympathizers, the Sheriff allowed visitors to see the gang after the convictions and sentencing. After only two days the Sheriff stopped the visiting. There were a minimum of 50 people at any given time trying to get in and see the gang. Family had priority.

This just got out of hand for the Sheriff. He couldn't control that many people all at once.

After he shut down visitation the Sheriff went to Cleon's cell to have a chat. The Sheriff took a liking to Cleon and would enter his cell and chat with him now and then. This time when the Sheriff entered the cell he noticed some shinny objects protruding from under the mattress He drew his gun on Cleon and ordered him back and down on his knees. The Sheriff reached under the bed and pulled out a dozen hacksaw blades, a pocket knife and a block of wood carved into the design of a cell key. He backed out of the cell and inserted the key in the lock and it nearly worked. He figured one more day of carving would make the key functional.

The Sheriff had enough of this gang. He called the State Highway Patrol and demanded that they get here and transport these people to prison. The MHP was there with ten squads within 3 hours and took the gang off to prison.

The Sheriff made a statement that arresting Saturday night drunks and settling family disputes would never be mundane again. He welcomed it.

Trial and Punishment

The stay in the Montevideo jail wouldn't be any easier than the night they already went through. They maybe would stay in the Montevideo jail, but they were going to be tried in a Benson court. Some people in Benson were having thoughts of lynching these crooks. Benson was the county seat for Swift County. For the most part, this county was a farming community and the banks were foreclosing on them as fast as paperwork could be generated. Not much money left over for an expensive trial. Hanging the gang would be cheaper.

When the gang made their first appearance in court, the caravan of police cars escorting the gang to Benson resembled a modern day presidential motorcade. There was a minimum of twenty heavily armed police and ten squad cars transporting the gang to Benson. It was a spectacular site for the citizens to observe.

The gang entered the courtroom and they were introduced to Judge Qvale. The gang heard the charges against them. The men were charged with armed robbery and the women were charged with kidnapping. One by one they pled not guilty. Not guilty? What were they thinking? Back to jail they went.

During the next few days the gang realized that their friends and family weren't going to rescue them. The jail was too fortified. During the next few days they each wrote and signed confessions to 63 crimes they committed during the last year. The confessions included the attempted armed robbery at Coggins.

They heard the rumors that on one of the trips to Benson some vigilantes were going to capture them and hang them. Not a great image in their minds. That also influenced their decision to plead guilty and take their chance on punishment. Another reason to plead guilty would perhaps be Minneapolis officials wouldn't prosecute them for the other crimes in Minneapolis.

A few days later they were transported to Benson with the caravan of lawmen. When they arrived at the courthouse there were a few hundred people lurking around the courthouse property. The lawmen didn't know what to think.

Were these people here to rescue the gang, or were they here to hang them? Taking no chances, the police drew their weapons and surrounded the gang as they entered the courtroom.

The courtroom was full. The judge warned everyone in the courtroom that any outburst would result in grave punishment by the court. He was ready to hear the pleadings from the defendants and he was also prepared to administer sentences.

First the men stood one at a time before the judge. Perley (Duco, Duke) Oliva pleads guilty to armed robbery in the 1st degree. Cleon Bonrud pleads guilty to armed robbery. Walter Christenson pleads guilty to armed robbery. Notice that they didn't plead to attempted armed robbery but rather 1st degree armed robbery.

The judge pronounced sentence. Each man was to serve 5-40 years at hard labor in the Stillwater State Prison.

Now the woman stood before the judge. Blanch Bonrud, Margaret Bonrud, and Mable Oliva all pled guilty to kidnapping. Blanch was sentenced to 5 years in the Shakopee Reformatory for Woman. Margaret was sentenced to 2 years in prison. Her sentence was stayed if she would enroll into the Big Sisters Institute for evaluation and treatment. The judge took pity on her for a couple reasons. First of all, it was her husband that was killed in the robbery. Second, she was only 18 years old and very naïve and impressionable. The judge thought she was miss-guided by her husband Nobel who filled her mind with criminal idealism. As it turned out, she couldn't be rehabilitated by the Big Sisters and was eventually sent to prison to serve her sentence.

Mable Oliva pleads guilty to kidnapping. She was sentenced to one year in Shakopee. When she heard the sentence she put on her drama queen act and fainted. She fell like a tree to the floor. The judge was not moved by her theatrics. She was determined to be the gangs' cheerleader and antagonist. Everyone thought she was a drama queen in everything she did. The truth be known, the gangsters were the only people that could tolerate her. Her family always thought she was too nutty and couldn't be trusted. She seldom told the truth. They knew she had become a prostitute before meeting Duco. They also knew she was a poor mother. She would constantly pass off the girls to relatives. Her own family was delighted that she would do prison time, they wouldn't have to put up with her and she had this coming for a long time. It was good riddance.

Her sentence was shorter because she had 2 daughters. With the state and counties being strapped for money it was thought by the judge that Mable should get out of prison sooner to raise her children. He did not favor the state to take custodial duty of these little girls.

He allowed Mable to make a choice as to whom and where the children can be taken while she served her sentence. After Mable regained her composure she requested that Mavis be taken to her sister Manda in Minneapolis. The six year old Darlos could be cared for with her sister Carrie in Montevideo. The judge ordered her request to be carried out immediately. The state police delivered the two girls to their respective temporary guardians.

The court proceedings were over. It was back to Montevideo. They would be held there until the State Police could arrange transportation to bring the gang to prison.

Stillwater Prison is located in Bayport, Minnesota. Bayport is a little town located next door to Stillwater, Minnesota. It was built in 1914 as a level 4 institution. The original prison was in Stillwater but it became obsolete. The prison population today is 1,381. Today the prison works as MINNCOR, Minnesota Corrections Industries. It supervises and designs a line of products that is tailor made for Minnesota state offices. They also produce signage, printing, furniture, and other products. The prison is a very intimidating structure when seen from the outside. Even though the prison offers tours, there are not many common citizen takers. The tours are usually for groups of delinquents that need the real shock value to be seen as their potential residence.

When Duke was committed to the prison April 12, 1933, the prison atmosphere at the time was somewhat darker. There were programs in place to help a prisoner learn an occupation but the occupations were probably a low paying variety. In 1933 prison was a place for punishment. They didn't coddle men back then. You did what they told you without question. If you refused the guards orders, corporal punishment would be dealt out. The bottom line back then was hard labor meant hard labor. Your civil rights were taken away. You had no recourse for what you might consider a wrong committed against you. You would grit your teeth and take it like a man. You have absolutely no control over your life in prison. Your choices are made by guards. You eat when they tell you to eat. You sleep when they tell you. You can't crap without the guards' permission. When outside your cell you are watched every second by someone.

The guards aren't the only ones watching you. Other prisoners with ulterior motives are watching you too. A wrong look could result in dire circumstances. In 1933 you had to really watch your backside for a number of reasons.

Cigarettes and toilet paper were the big ticket items. Inmates would fight over these items or use them as barter power for other things. One thing Duke had going for himself, he stood 6'1" at about 200 pounds.

He always had a scowl on his face. He was a mean looking SOB. There is nothing in his prison records that indicate any problems he may have had with others. Besides, his partners in crime were also in the same prison. Cleon and Walter were formidable men to challenge. They've been in prison before. In St. Cloud, Minnesota there is a prison that is even more intimidating than Stillwater. Stillwater was modern compared to St. Cloud and I think Cleon and Walter thought it was a paradise by comparison. Without any records of misbehavior, I'm assuming that the three of them got along with other inmates and didn't experience any problems.

The only exception I found about Duke is that he experienced severe stomach cramps on occasion and he would land in the infirmary for treatment. Duco's life in prison seemed to be somewhat comfortable. He performed electrical duties such as wiring machines, new rooms, and he worked on major electrical tools. Prior to being enrolled in the Bonrud Gang he was an electrician working for a contractor named John Christenson. John always liked Duke. He literally took him under his wing and guided him through his apprenticeship and into his journeyman status. Prior to his arrest John was paying Duke $200.00 a week. In 1933 that was excellent money and it afforded him luxuries that a lot of people of the day considered frivolous.

Duco had been divorced from his previous wife June for several years. She was constantly complaining about the low wage Duco was receiving while in prison. His paycheck from prison amounted to $30-35.00 a month. June would receive half of that amount for child support and alimony. Now that's a huge difference from what he was paying before his arrest. Another strange thing I noticed about her was her frequent visits to Duco in prison. She was the one that initiated their divorce, but she couldn't stay away from him.

Duco had been married to the rabble rouser Mable for about 2 years prior to their imprisonment. Mable was informed that June was visiting her husband. Now I'm here to tell you, that didn't settle well with Mable and the one thing you shouldn't do is piss off Mable. She was serving her time in the woman's Shakopee facility. This is a little town seated along the Minnesota River about 15 miles southwest of Minneapolis. Savage, Minnesota is its neighbor. Savage was the birth place for the famous trotting hoarse, Dan Patch.

This correction facility in Shakopee resembles a hospital more than a prison. It sits on 167 acres and it is a three story building. At one time the prisoners raised pigs, chickens and cows. An interesting fact about the prison is the fact that it has never had a wall around it or any kind of fence.

Mable had a tougher time adjusting to prison life. Her arrogance always landed her in hot water with the guards. She would claim she was convicted by accident and she shouldn't be in prison. She didn't make any friends. In fact, a lot of her time in prison was in protective custody because of her drama queen attitude towards other inmates. The guards couldn't stand her. She thought she was better than anyone in that facility.

What I find ironic about her is when some other inmate was just about ready to pound her to pieces; she would tell the person that her gang wouldn't take kindly to her being beat up. Great harm or death could visit her tormenter sooner or later. Her mistaken guilty plea goes out the window when she admits to her association with the gang. She wasn't very smart.

As a pass time she would sew dresses for her daughters in her spare time. Her youngest is pictured in one of these dresses. It's the only one she received. The guards hated Mable so much, when she gave the guards the packaged dress to mail to her daughter, the guard would either take the dress home for their child or just throw it away. Mable wasn't well liked by anyone. Even Blanch and Margaret wouldn't associate with her. All this dislike and hatred had to wear on Mable. I believe it made her even bitterer than what she was before prison. Some of the bitterness can be seen in letters to Duco and the warden. Mable sent a blistering letter to the Stillwater warden demanding that she should receive half of what June received for child support. She also demanded that June stay away from her husband. The warden agreed to limit the visitation but he wouldn't allow payments to Mabel for child support. Mable's children were not Duco's.

These were the behaviors of my grandparents while in prison. Duco was able to adjust to prison life, and Mable couldn't. Of coarse Duco was going to spend more time in prison so he had no choice but to adjust. Mable just had to limp through a year. I would venture a guess that Mable would have been eliminated if her sentence was longer. Inmates and guards hated her that much. I believe Duco got along with nearly everyone he met in prison. When he wanted to be a nice person, he could bring it out of himself.

Mabel did her time and was released after her year sentence. She was one bitter person. She was holding a grudge against the Stillwater warden and she wasn't happy with Duco receiving his ex wife many times during the past year. Her mission was to get to Stillwater and raise hell with those people. That's exactly what she did. If there is one thing that woman good do well, it was to piss other people off.

You would think that she would want to see her two daughters first. Not so. She was primed for a fight. She arrived at Stillwater the day after her release. After signing in the visitors' book her first order of business was to examine the guest register.

Sure enough, June's name was still showing up as recent as the week before. Now she was boiling over. She demanded to see the warden. She made a scene until the warden became available.

The warden welcomed her into his office and asked her how he could help her. She laid into him about his broken word to keep June away from her husband. Next, she had information that June had remarried and her present husband makes excellent money. Mable demanded that the alimony be stopped and given to her instead. She also wanted more than the meager 15 minutes for visitation with her husband.

The warden felt like he just got run over by a truck. All he could say was that he would take these issues seriously and get her answers by next week. She wanted to visit with the three men in her life while she was there. The warden would allow only one prisoner per visit. It was policy and he couldn't change it. She agreed and wanted a half hour with Duco. The warden approved her request for a half hour.

Later the warden heard from a head guard. The guard stated that when Mable met with Duco the conversation was all hers. He didn't get a word in at all. He got a royal chewing out. When she left, the guard said the room was so cold a refrigerator would blush. Duco was left at the table seated and bent over with his head in his hands. He was embarrassed and frustrated.

Duco was remembering conversations he had with his boss John Christenson. John told Duco that Mable was no good for him. He should just divorce her and get some distance between them. She was a bad influence and she would eventually get him in trouble. Now he was in prison and just got chewed out by a woman. It was a scene he will never live down with his fellow inmates. He would be teased to no end about this day. He was whipped.

The following week Mable got the reply from the warden. He agreed on all counts except one. He wouldn't split the spousal support with her and June. Mable was furious but she knew there was no appealing the warden's decision.

From that day on, Mable would visit the prison once a week. She would alternate visits between Duco and her brother Cleon. On an off week, I wonder, just how relieved that person felt knowing that she wouldn't be asking for him.

Duco had a variety of visitors while in prison. Of coarse June would still see Duco. Mable was informed that if June brought their two children for a visit, she wouldn't be denied the visit. Several of Mable's brothers and sisters also visited Duco.

His parents and siblings were also frequent visitors. A big surprise was the several visits from the Minnesota Bureau of Criminal Apprehension lead investigator, Melvin Passholt. These visits were curious indeed. Duco was liked by most people he met.

Duco was a decent fellow until he hooked up with Mable. His only fault is that he was the last one to figure this out. When he did, it was too late.

Duco would spend 5 more years in the Stillwater Prison. In some weird way the prison sentence seemed preferable than the sentence he had with Mable. Now that she was out of prison, Mable needed a place to live and a job to pay the rent. Her two daughters were with relatives and she wasn't all that concerned about their well being.

Mable had an 8th grade education. Not enough schooling to get her any kind of good paying job. The current economic depression was holding low grade employment down. People had very little if any disposable money for movies, department stores or even eating out in a restaurant. She finally found employment with the help of the Little Sisters Organization. She would be working in two different café's washing dishes part time. They also managed to find her a cheap one room apartment.

It was a struggle for her to make ends meet. The café's would allow her to take home left over food and other charity groups in Minneapolis would help with clothing. Life was tough on an ex con with little education. As hard as things were for her at this time, she learned to keep her mouth shut around her employers. She didn't want to risk loosing her jobs. She worked hard at the café's and barely kept up with her bills. She managed to stash away just enough money for a bus ride to Stillwater once a week to see her men.

When she was visiting the boys at the prison, her attitude would change back to the wicked old lady everyone grew to hate. On visiting day the guards and even the warden would bead up some sweat when she arrived. That woman just can't be nice. Why does Duco put up with her? To understand their relationship is to understand their desires. Mable was always on the look out for a stable man that would be a good provider. She would do anything to land such a man.

Duco was an over sexed beer drinking fool. Most of his thinking beyond electricity was from below his belt. He couldn't get enough sex. He couldn't drink enough beer either. When they met, Mable was already an experienced prostitute and Duco was a man with a great job. Even divorced he was able to afford another family. They were the perfect match.

Mable had her two daughters, Mavis and Darlos. Duco took to them easily and didn't even flinch when he and Mable married in Wisconsin. They played hard together. Every now and then they would distribute the girls to relatives so they could go on a drunken sex trip sometimes lasting for days.

They had rented an apartment at 1211 Franklin Avenue in Minneapolis. This place turned out to be a gathering place for Mable's brothers and their wives. These people would get together and party for days. The liquor and beer was endless and so was the sex. On Friday and Saturday nights they would go to the local dance hall and dance the night away. When the dance hall closed they would walk the couple blocks home and continue with their party for a couple days.

After a few days of partying Cleon would excuse the original gang members from Duco and Mable's hospitality and just disappear for several days. While they were gone Duke and Mable would hop in Duco's car and gather up the girls. Mavis was in Minneapolis with her aunt Manda. They would retrieve her first. Darlos was in Montevideo with her aunt Carrie and Uncle Fred. It would be a day trip to pick her up. They usually had a good time on the farm.

Montevideo tired the family. They would spend the night and head for Minneapolis in the morning. At this time Mavis was 11 years old and Darlos was 5 years old. I believe it's now it should be said that Darlos was spending most of her life with Carrie and Fred. Darlos was born from prostitution and Mable always called her the unwanted child. She would leave her with her sister every chance she could get. If staying with just Carrie alone, Darlos would have been fine. She was constantly molested from the age of 4 up to her teen age years by her deviant uncle.

It would surface years later when Darlos would finally start objecting his passes and start complaining to Carrie.

The story of her molestation took an evil turn when she reported it to her mother. One day when she was around 10 years old, Darlos built up enough courage to tell her mother about uncle's advances and touching. Mable blew up at her. What are you doing to make him come at you like that? Are you teasing him? You're wearing makeup, aren't you? What ever your doing that makes him want you; you had better stop. It's your fault, not his. You better not bring this up again.

I believe my mother's story about this molesting 100%. Her whole life was scared by this. It came up in many conversations with her and obliquely with Mavis. I have even recently heard that Darlos would constantly ask other friends and relatives to take her in. At the time the family was afraid of the gang and didn't want them to have any excuse for them to visit. Having Darlos would give the gang that excuse.

This of coarse was a disaster for Darlos. Her mother blamed her for his sickness. Who can she turn to now? She imagined Carrie would react the same way. She didn't get along well enough with Duco and he was in prison anyhow. She really didn't know anyone else. She would just have to beg her mother to stay in Minneapolis.

That eventually is what happened. Darlos was finally able to stay with her mother. She jumped out of the pan and into the fire.

By now Mable resorted back to her old ways of making money. Duco still had a few years to serve in prison and Mable was tired of cleaning dishes. She would entertain her customers in the same bed Darlos would be sleeping in. This was a one room apartment with just one bed. Her customers would do unimaginable things in that bed with Mable and little Darlos.

Mable also became very proficient at extortion. She would gain the confidence of a customer through sex. At first she charged him for her service and on subsequent dates she would give it away gaining his affection. Eventually the fellow would invite her and the girls to stay with him in his home. Mable would move in and play the perfect mate and house keeper. The larceny in her heart would eventually overcome her.

She would leave for a few days at a time and come back looking like she fell out of a garbage truck. It was obvious that she was out performing her profession. The man of the house would get upset and threaten to kick her out. Mable was good at what she did professionally and apply her talent on him and smooth things over.

After a while the man would notice items missing from his house. Some things were expensive, and others were keepsakes. He knew what was happening. He called for Mable. She came to him and received the beating of her life. He told her to get out or he would call the cops. Mable picked herself up and gathered her things and the girls and left. She still had her one room apartment to live in.

Over a period of five years she stayed with several men under those circumstances. It would last a couple months before she got itchy feet and had to walk out. She had ample opportunity to divorce

Duco and marry a well to do man. Deep down, she missed the excitement of being with Duke.

During April of 1939 Duco was attending his parole hearings. At the meetings was John Christenson. He was there for Duco as a supporter and an employer. John told the review committee that Duco will work full time for him. He would help set him up with a place to live and would do his best to keep Duco on the straight and narrow.

He just had one worry to express to the board. He thought the marriage to Mable was a mistake and in his opinion Duco should divorce her and stay away from her. He would have a better chance of succeeding in life without her.

Funny thing; most of the people on the board have either heard of Mable or have had a run in with her. The chairman asked Duco what his thoughts were about this matter.

He said that he would do whatever the board recommends. The board added to the normal restrictions, Duco shall not associate himself with Mable while on parole. If Duco agreed to this, he would be paroled. He agreed. Parole was granted May 29, 1939. He was a free man with heavy restrictions.

When Mable found out about the restriction she went crazy. Letters by the dozens went out to the parole board and warden. How could they interfere with a marriage?

She had a point, but nobody was listening. John picked Duco up from prison. It's been a long time since he rode in a car. The air smelled better outside the gate too. The gray appearance of things now has color again. Trees are a wonder to see.

Duco Is Freed

Duco was a semi free man again. Life on parole would certainly present him with serious challenges. John had set him up in a decent apartment near downtown Minneapolis. True to his word to the parole board, John kept Duco very busy with work. Until Duco could afford a car John would pick him up from work every day and bring him home at quitting time. Duco had temptations to face every day. His parole conditions were;

1. No alcohol (liquor or beer)
2. No consorting with ex convicts or questionable people.
3. No entering establishments that serve alcohol.
4. No possession of any kind of weapon. (Guns and knives longer than 3")
5. No home loans
6. No car loans
7. No loans of any kind. All items must be purchased with cash.

8. Must be in his home between 9:00 PM – 6:00 AM unless under supervised work projects.
9. Refrain visitation and phone calls from Mable Oliva.
10. Visit parole officer as directed with a once a week minimum.

Yes, these rules were going to be challenging. For one thing, beer was a weakness. So was sex. Granted, he's been without his favorite vises for 6 years. He should have these problems solved and behind him. He figured that work would keep his mind off these habits. He asked John for more and more overtime. John just loved that mans work ethics. He gave him all the work he wanted. Business was good for John. Everyone wanted electricity in their homes. Factories were upgrading electrical machinery with money from President Roosevelt's' "New Deal". Any contractor with any kind of vision for the future could make a business killing right now. Duco had the right knowledge for the right times. He again was making a minimum of $200.00 a week. His overtime was bringing in another $100-150.00 a week. This wage was money fit for a King.

Before Duco knew what hit him, he had his own apartment with new furniture, radio and a new car. He paid cash for everything. He was current with his parole officer and was given excellent grades by him. Life was going extremely good for Duke. His temptations were under control thanks to the extra work that John handed him. His days were full of work. On his own time he learned how to grocery shop and shop for new cloths. He even learned how to cook. In the evening he enjoyed listening to his Hi-Fi Radio. He purchased nothing but the newest and best products. He could afford it.

Cleon had passed his parole review a few days later than Duco. They both got out of prison on the same day but at different times.

Even though they were brother-in-laws, contact between them was prohibited. Cleon had divorced his wife while in prison.

He had the same parole conditions as Duco with the exception of the "Mable" clause. Cleon would meet up with Mable and the party would start all over again. This time there would be no road trips.

For about 6 months Mable and Duco were separated by parole rules. It was starting to wear thin. At night Duco would imagine her next to him and Mable, well who knows what she was thinking? I suspect she was dreaming about a stable relationship with the man bringing in a good income. I think sex was a meaningless act for her now. She was so prolific at prostitution that I tend to believe she had no sensual feelings at all.

The saying goes, "All good things must come to an end." With Duco it came to an end with a phone call. It was Mable. Duco heard her voice and he developed goose bumps. All his guards were dropped instantly. Mable said she was thinking about him. He said she was on his mind every night. The conversation lasted a long time. There was a lot of catching up to do. Towards the end of the conversation they discussed the possibility of getting together. Duco told her that he could loose his freedom if they were seen together. If they meet, it has to be done discretely. They continued with that train of thought until they talked each other into a rendezvous. Duco told her about his apartment. He stated that nobody ever checks up on him while he's at home. It would be safe for her to meet him here. She agreed to meet him the next evening after dark.

The next day at work was the longest day Duco ever put in. His normal 8 hour day felt like 16 hours. When quitting time came he shot himself to the grocery store and picked up some romantic dinner items. He rushed home and did a whirlwind house cleaning and then began to cook supper. He would be expecting her around 7:00 PM.

It was now 5:30 PM. He was making a roast beef dinner with all the trimmings. He went as far as to buy candles for the table. The only thing missing was a nice wine. He wouldn't risk trying alcohol. He figured once he started, he wouldn't stop.

Mable was on her way to Duco's house. She was totally broke. Her thoughts of meeting Duco were completely different. She was going there to ask for money.

When she found out about his financial wealth, she thought she should have a piece of the action. After all, they are still married. She arrived at 7:00 PM sharp. Once Duco opened the door to let her in, both of them instantly dropped their defenses and thoughts and ran directly to the bedroom. How do I know all this? Keep reading.

After several hours of sex and a burned roast beef the pillow talk started. Mable didn't believe the parole board had the authority to separate a wedded couple. She thought that the constitution protected her with the separation of church and state.

With that condition imposed on their relationship it sure had the odor of the state dictating how a lawful married couple with religious sanctions. Duco said he thought that his civil rights are taken away while serving his sentence. Parole is still part of the judge's sentence. That is true, but how can that rule apply to Mable? She served her full term and received her certificate from the Governor restoring her civil rights. Mable thought that they could win there objection to this rule in court.

Duco was getting a bit scared now. He didn't like the idea of going to court for any reason. His last court appearance wasn't such a pleasant experience. A judge threw the book at him. Mable turned out to be very persuasive. She said they would take baby steps in reviving their relationship. A night here, a night there, and a week stay here and there, and then one day they will move in. Duco couldn't refuse.

He wanted her back at any cost. The next morning Mable left before Duco went to work. She would be back in a couple days.

That day at work Duco had a spring in his step and a grin on his face. John noticed the improved mood and asked Duco what was making him so happy. Duco was speechless. He told John that he would let him know later. Duco either had to tell the truth or come up with some fantastic lie. John wouldn't accept Mable under any condition, he hated her.

In mid 1940 Duco and Mable started seeing each other in Duco's apartment. These were clandestine meetings. They wanted to keep their getting back together secret from Duco's boss, John. Surely if John was to find out about them getting back together, he would run straight to the parole officer. This would be a violation of Duco's parole terms and he could be sent back to Stillwater and forced to serve out the rest of his 5-40 year sentence. He had already served 7 years with one year being on parole. The thought of serving 33 years just about makes him want to puke. That is a high price to pay for sex.

These two people were so blinded by there individual needs they didn't stop to think about the violation. Their blindness also made them careless. One night while Mable was there for a visit John stopped by to talk with Duco about an up coming project. After John knocked on the door and Duco answered it, the door was open enough for John see Mable in a nightgown sitting on the couch. Actually, John wasn't all that surprised. At least he didn't show it. He handed Duco some blue prints and said that he would talk to him tomorrow. John left without another word. Duco nearly had to change his pants. He went over to the couch and plopped down next to Mable. They couldn't get the words out. They just sat there.

The next day Duke reported for work and John was there waiting for him. John said he needed to talk and he said they could eat out for breakfast on him. Duco has known John for many years and one thing is certain about John. Usually when he takes an employee out for breakfast, it's to get their walking papers. Duco saw his comfortable life flash before his eyes. He also heard the sound of metallic jail doors slamming behind him. Yep, he thought John was going to fire him. Then he was going to report him to his parole officer. After that, back to Stillwater. He was screwed by Mable last night, and now he's getting screwed by John this morning. He got into John's car for the ride to a café. John never said a word during the 10 minute ride.

When they arrived at the café John requested a table away from any people. He told the waitress that they needed privacy to discuss business. After they were seated they both ordered breakfast and coffee. As the waitress walked away John turned to Duke and said, "What the hell were you thinking?" John said that he was obligated by law to report his infraction to his parole officer. He explained to Duco that he could loose his business if he didn't report the violation.

It was just too much for John to loose. He had several other employees that depend on him to find work so they can raise their families. He wasn't going to allow anyone, including a friend of several years, destroy those families because Duco wants to get laid. John wanted to know what makes her so special. What is it about her that makes you risk going to prison for 33 years. Duco would start to answer and John would keep coming up with questions.

Finally a moment of silence came over both of them. After a moment Duco said he had no excuse. He just wanted John to understand that they are a married couple and it was a clergy ceremony as prescribed by law. They are a legally married couple and it's believed that the parole board over stepped their authority in banning their relationship.

Duco understood that his civil rights have been taken away, but Mables have been restored. He feels that the parole board is violating her constitutional rights by not keeping church and state separate. Her sins to the state have been paid in full and now the state is discriminating against her for being loud and boisterous. That could be a violation of her freedom of speech. Oh boy, did Duco lay it on thick.

John acknowledged his point of view but he still had the problem of the mandatory reporting a parole violation. He can't escape that. He told Duco that his job is safe and firing him wouldn't help either one of them. He was an exceptional electrician and couldn't be replaced. Even though he didn't like Mable he would talk with the parole officer and state Duco's case.

Later that day John called the parole officer and told him about the violation he witnessed. The parole officer wanted to know what John thought would be Duco's next move. John thought that they were both going to be more discreet. The parole officer gave John a bit of information that could possibly bust up the couple for good.

He told John to keep an eye on them, and if she shows up again, call him and he will go talk with Duco and bring out a secret weapon. John asked "Why wait? If you have a secret weapon now would be a great time to bring it out. Duco is scared out of his wits right now. It's a perfect time to scare him straight." The parole officer agreed. He asked John if he would like to join him. John said he would. They would wait until Duco was home from work.

Later that day Duco arrived home. Mable had gone back to her apartment for a few days, so he was alone and worried about what the parole officer would do to him. It's been a real dumper of a day.

About a half hour later there was a knock at the door. Duke knew who it was. He answered the door and let John and the parole officer in. They gathered in the living room. John apologized to Duco for having to bring the parole officer in with him. He also told Duco he would gladly keep him on as an employee if the parole officer let him slip this mistake by.

The parole officer started making his case with Duco. He pointed out that he did violate the terms of his parole and he could be sent back to prison. He pointed out one thing that put Duco at ease. If he was going to violate his terms and return him to prison, he would have brought several police officers with him to place him under arrest. There were no police in sight. Duco took a deep breath of relief.

The parole officer continued with telling Duco that he knew of a problem with Mabel that he thought would be relevant to the situation today. While you two have been seeing each other for the last few months, Mable had another man she was satisfying on the side. She was living with an Arnold Christenson and they were playing house together.

That took the breath out of both Duco and John! The parole officer told Duco that Mable has been under observation for several months. A few of the "Johns" she was shacking up lately were gangsters from outside Minnesota. Now she hasn't done anything as bad as before, and even though prostitution is illegal, the authorities were leaving her alone with these criminal elements.

If the gangsters are preoccupied, they may just leave town without causing any trouble. So far this has worked. The gang activity in Minneapolis and St. Paul has dropped. They weren't sure how many prostitutes were working these gangsters, but it appears it's just right.

The parole officer left Duco with one final thought. He disagreed with the restraining order. He said that you're married and the parole board had no right to issue that restraint. He will not violate Duco for being with his wife. In fact, because of his excellent behavior, he was going to recommend complete prison release to the governor.

This floored Duco and John. They were both at a loss for words. On one hand Duco was mad as hell with Mable but elated that he may get a total release. Duco thought out loud that he was done with that two timing bitch Mable. He couldn't believe that she was whispering all those sweet nothings in his ears. It must have been practice for her "Johns" later. How could he be taken in so deep? She was a pro! Scamming people is what she does best.

What Duco failed to see was Mabel's formative years. Cleon was in the St. Cloud prison for grand larceny. He got out when Mable was at an age when she was most impressionable. She had just moved to Minneapolis and she hooked up with Cleon and Walter. Later her other larceny filled brother Nobel would join them in Minneapolis. Mable learned from the best. They all chummed around with each other until it came time for the Bonrud gang to ride. Mable wasn't allowed to join them on their crime sprees. She was just too young. When they came back they would brag about the crimes they committed. Mable wasn't asked to join the gang until after she married Duco.

They were both invited to join in their sprees during the late months of 1931. By the time Mable joined the gang, she was a professional prostitute. She had been selling herself since 1926. She even bore a child from a "John". She was a con artist and also knew how to handle a gun. Her knowledge of crime was equal to Duco's knowledge of electricity. This woman was bad.

When all the talk was finally over, the two men left Duke with his thoughts. He sure has a lot to think about. Duco thanked them for stopping by and led them out the door. He was thankful that he wasn't going back to prison, but for some weird reason all that talk about Mable turned him on. He would take a nap and wake up with a fresh mind.

His nap lasted all night. He woke up early with his mind cleared. He wondered if yesterday was a dream or did he hear the parole agent right? Was he really going to recommend total release? Oh happy days! Now, what about Mable? I need to have a talk with her. The parole agent even gave a green light on us being together. I can get over her sins. We just need to talk. He wondered if he would have to kill that guy she was shacking up with. Wow, so many questions.

That night with John and the parole officer was a memory. He just let his thoughts about Mable stall. It's been a few months since that conversation. It was now late April, 1941. He had a new car that he paid cash for, and he was always looking at new electronics to buy. He heard about television by reading articles sent to him in the mail. He will be buying the first one that comes out. Things of any electronic nature fascinated him. John was still giving him all the hours he wanted. In fact, he had become the lead electrician and joined the new union. John promoted him to foreman. He would receive $1.50 above senior wages for these duties.

It's been a few months since he heard from Mable. He thought about her often but he also looked at how much strain has been relieved by not seeing her. His life was cruising very smooth right now. His parole agent kept completing forms in favor of his attitude and behavior. He was getting high marks all the way around. Again, life was good.

May 1st he received a call from his parole agent that paperwork has been submitted to the Department of Corrections pronouncing him rehabilitated and he should be totally released from his sentence.

He figured it should be approved within a couple weeks. There is no need to report to him anymore. He wished Duco the best of luck and hung up.

Sure enough, during the first week in May he received his official release forms from DOC and also enclosed was an official document with the great seal of Minnesota affixed at the top. It was the most important paper of them all. It had the Governor's signature affixed announcing that his United States Civil Rights have been completely restored. He can vote again, get a home mortgage, have a beer, and do whatever a normal citizen can do. He was elated. In fact the first thing he was going to do was take his guardian angel John out for a beer. He called him and John accepted. The two had a great night out. Duco owed it all to him. Life was moving along very well for Duco. He had purchased a house in south Minneapolis. It was a good feeling to have a mortgage. He owned his own property for the first time in his life. He really liked his house. It even had a garage for his car. Duco was on top of the world.

It had to come eventually. Mable called in a panic and said that Arnold was threatening her with a gun. She claimed he was going to kill her. Duco told her to do her best to hang on, he would call the police.

When the police arrived, Arnold had Mable on the ground outside and was sitting on her with a knife to her throat. The police drew their guns and ordered him to stop. When he looked up he saw several guns pointed at his head. He gave up. Mable was released. Arnold was arrested and charged with aggravated assault and jailed. He would later be found guilty and serve 5 years in prison.

A short time later Duco showed up at her house. She was still shaking from fear. He did everything he could to comfort her. Little did they know this was the beginning of their lives together. A few days after that incident, Mable gathered everything she owned and Darlos and moved into Duco's new house. It was the honeymoon they never had.

It was late 1941 and Mavis had been married and out of the house. She had two children of her own. There were problems in her marriage and she would eventually divorce and re-marry. Darlos was working as a waitress making her own spending money.

The trips to Montevideo had stopped a few years ago. Up until the time that Arnold was around, Darlos would just stay away from home when her mother entertained the "Johns". The sexual abuse she went through for nearly 15 year had stopped. She got along with Duco but with caution. Since the abuses she suffered from her uncle and her mother's customers, she found it hard to trust any man not her age.

Duco had what he wanted now. It was a built in family that he could care for and a wife that gave him sexual pleasures beyond his wildest dreams. What he liked most of all was his freedom. It was time to put all that gangster stuff behind him. Everything was going smooth. They were enjoying the comforts that each of them offered each other. It was back to the basics. Duco received the sex he always wanted and Mable received the security she always wanted.

Everything was good on the surface. As time went by trouble in paradise would bubble up. They would have arguments that would rattle the walls. Their real personalities were starting to clash. For the next few years life at the Oliva home was tense at times and romantic at other times. Duco was working every bit as hard in 1945 as he did in 1939. He was still making a great wage. He had his television and he bought a new Cadillac every two years. He was now exploring the idea of being a landlord.

Duco sold the house to Mavis and her new husband Omar. He financed it for them with an interest bearing loan. This rate was higher than bank rates back then, but the banks were very tight with handing out mortgages. Omar was fine with the payments. He was employed at the St. Paul Ford plant. He installed the rear axel assembly on the line.

At that time the United Auto Workers union was young and wages were depressed. Omar still had enough to make house payments to Duco but that was about it. Ford certainly didn't give any breaks to employees on discounts. Things at Ford changed from the time when old man Ford would offer his employees specials on purchases. Omar owned Fords. Eventually Omar would earn a salary that allowed him to obtain a bank mortgage and pay off the loan he had with Duco.

You have to give credit to Duco. He drew up the mortgage papers. Every word he put in that contract was to his favor. If a payment was 5 days late, he would foreclose on the house. The occupant would have to move out with out any recourse. Who ever borrowed money from Duco had better exhausted every other resource. His terms were extremely strict. He would get his money back, one way or another.

Duco purchased an eight unit apartment building just a few blocks from his house. He was in his glory now. He was a landlord and he was a strict landlord. The building was a white stucco flat top structure. It had a single car garage that housed his Cadillac.

Being the electrician that he is, he was among the first in Minneapolis to have an electric garage door opener. He was extremely happy with this toy and like showing it off to his friends.

As the 1940's progressed, WW2 was the big threat to the peace and prosperity of every USA citizen. Our country was transformed overnight from a producer of consumer goods to a producer of war materials. Our young men were enlisting and being drafted into the armed services by the thousands. They were fighting and dying by the thousands too.

These years weren't talked about. The war took the effort of every citizen to either fight or contribute time and money to the war machine. My mother wouldn't talk much about their lives going through the war other than to say that she worked for the Donaldson Company producing some kind of electrical components for war equipment. She talked about the rations for food and gas she said that they still lived with a modest amount of comfort. I know my mother had friends she associated with at malt shops. She didn't do much dating until the war was nearly over. I think the war overwhelmed and overtook the minds and souls of the American public.

The war was filled with daily horrors of our boys being killed and wounded on the battlefields in the Pacific Islands and in the European theater of battle.

Our radio programs were loaded with patriotic songs and pleas to buy war bonds. News was seldom good. Hitler was creating hot spots on every border in Europe. The talk of Tiger tanks and secret weapons with rockets dropping out of space was scaring the hell out of us. German submarines were sinking ships off our coastline.

We finally had our confidence lifted on June 6, 1944, D-Day when our armed forces finally started to get the upper hand on the German Army. On the other side of the world our soldiers were fighting island to island to stop the advancing Japanese Army. 1945 proved to be the year of victory. Germany surrendered May 8, 1945 and Japan surrendered August 14, 1945. The free world overcame the threat of dictatorship and crushed the opposing Armies world wide.

With the wars end came a bunch of sex crazed soldiers home to their sweethearts. GI's that didn't have a sweetheart found one real quick, because the girls were waiting for them. My mother was waiting for her sweetheart as much as anyone. Darlos didn't have to wait long. Jack Halverson came along and blew her away.

They dated frequently during late 1945 and married in January 1946. Duco put on a grand wedding for them. It was perhaps one of his greatest moments with Darlos. They came together for just that brief time and let down their defenses and accepted each other as family. I could tell they were happy by the photographs taken at the wedding. With both of her daughters married off, Mable now had Duco all to herself. I don't think either one of them were extremely enthused about that idea. They have been married for a number of years now and they have been living under the same roof for about six years. They have been through trials and challenges nobody else could survive.

Yes, looking back at all the troubles they went through and the suffering they endured, it was time for payback. They were about to become the poster child for how couples with shady pasts can argue. Their fights would be legendary. They defined abuse.

Now that Jack and Darlos were married the realization of living in an empty nest struck Mable and Duke. They were fighting with each other over everything. According to my dad, these fights were explosive. They would start their fights in bed after sex. It would start off as pillow talk. It would escalate into an argument and then they would both get out of bed and get into a fist fight. After the fist fight one of them would end up on the couch for the night. They were both physically hard on each other and quite capable of bruising each other. When the next morning came around, they would both be sporting black eyes. This usually sent a message to settle down for a few days.

Mable was able to stay home and hide her black eye, but Duco had to go to work. Many times he had to come up with a false story about his black eye. How could he tell anyone that his wife popped him in the eye?

Duco was a beer drinker extraordinaire. He could pack away a case of beer a day along with 3-4 packs of cigarettes. Drinking a couple beers on the job back then was acceptable to John. As long as Duco didn't get drunk and abusive, a few beers are ok.

I'm not sure of the exact date, but during the very late 1940's after Darlos's wedding, Duco left John Christenson Electrical Contractors and went to work for the Grain Belt Brewery in Minneapolis. The brewery was off Marshall Avenue and Broadway. Leaving John was hard for Duco but he needed a job that had some benefits and a retirement plan. It should be said that second to beer, money was the most important thing in his life. He had the Midas touch when it came to investing for his future.

His bank account was growing from the apartment building revenue. He certainty didn't loose any money moving to Grain Belt. With his knowledge of electricity he was the lead electrician.

He was in the United Electrical Workers Union and being the lead electrician endowed him extra pay per hour and most importantly, he was the number one man for trouble shooting after hours. The trouble shooting was Duco's golden goose. After he was home for the day Duco was on call for any electrical problems. It could be just a fuse blown out, but the night foreman had to call Duco in to replace it. He lived 20 minutes away from the brewery. When he got a call he would go to the brewery, flip a switch and go home. This usually lasted an hour all together.

He would get paid for a 4 hour minimum with double time! There were times when he would be called in a couple times in one night. Every phone call paid the same. He was so well paid at the brewery he could buy a new Cadillac every year and pay cash. It was the only Cadillac in the employee's parking lot. Out of all the labor force at the brewery, Duco was the highest paid union employee. He was making a killing. Mable's wish for a man with a good income came true. What also made this a dream job for Duco; in his shop was a faucet that poured beer. Yes, as long as the employee remained in control of himself, drinking beer on the job was acceptable. Between the night calls and the up-keep on the apartment building, Duke was getting worn out. Something had to give. He decided to sell the apartment building.

They discovered a very nice house at 43rd and Portland Ave. So., in south Minneapolis. It was the perfect home for them. It was a corner lot and the garage had room for two cars and its driveway was on 43rd Street. This house was setup with two bedrooms on the main floor and two more up stairs. It had a mud room, very fancy for the time period, and it doubled as a 4 season porch. The kitchen was large with a breakfast nook and the dining room was huge. The living room was a very nice size and it had a fireplace. The basement was plumbed for a toilet. Mable boasted that the picture window was the largest in the twin cities. I don't know about that, but it was huge.

Duco made a fine profit on the sale of the apartment building. In fact, he was doing so well financially, he was able to pay mostly cash for the new house. He had little or no need for a mortgage. Once in their new home their attitudes took a turn for the worse. I was around 5 years old and I remember visiting them and the sense of high tension filling the house. It's hard to explain, but even at that age things just didn't feel right. It was like a monarchy was proclaimed.

At the time we were living in a rented home in Minnetonka, Minnesota. In 1952 dad and mom packed up everything in a truck and moved us to our new home in Bloomington, Minnesota. It was 1952. Dad was extremely happy with this house. It was a three bedroom rambler seated on a ¾ acre lot. It was part of a new housing community in a suburb located 15 miles south of Minneapolis. They were cookie cutter houses. In this area alone there had to be several hundred of them built.

We were now part of the new fad called, "Suburban Dwellers". Most of these homes were purchased by the WW2 veterans under a new veteran home mortgage program. Most veteran guaranteed loans were set at a very low interest rate and in most cases no down payment was required.

This veteran mortgage program helped boost home building nation wide. The number of homes being built was beyond the Washington DC economics expert's wildest dreams. Houses couldn't be built fast enough and construction workers were being schooled in numbers equal to the home development. That was also thanks to the Veterans Admin. They also would pay for the veterans schooling. My dad took his place in these benefits by attending Dunwoody Trade School and learning heating and air conditioning installation. He also was a hard wood floor installer. He had to drop installing floors when he went through his 2 year apprenticeship in sheet metal.

In the beginning things were very tight for dad. The sheet metal union was in its infancy and wages were very low. Even when he became a journeyman his wage didn't increase much. Bringing up four kids was expensive in the suburbs. Dad went back to laying floors as a second job. He would also install gutters on private homes on weekends. Even with all this extra work, money was tight.

In the late 1950's, the union voted to go on strike for higher wages. They demanded equal pay with the electrical, plumbers, and carpenter unions. This was a devastating strike. It would last for weeks. Dad took out a personal loan with one of those high interest scam artist loan places. These loan outfits gave money to anyone. The borrower would literally sign all their personal property over to the loan company as collateral. It included everything you owned. If you skipped a payment for any reason, even if you were deathly sick in the hospital, they would put your loan in default and collect their collateral. This could include you house and car. At the time there were very little federal or state regulations controlling these legalized thieves. Some of them are still around today.

My dad was in this loan trap. The strike wasn't even close to settling when his payments started to come due. Laying floors wasn't enough money to pay the bills. He couldn't install gutters while the strike was going on. It was sheet metal work. Dad was about to loose everything. He couldn't let that happen. His only coarse of relief was to borrow money from Duco. This was the hardest decision that dad and mom ever had to make. They knew how hard Duco was on Mavis and Omar with their home loan and the interest they had to pay.

The strike was in its 5th week with no settlement in sight. Dad figured the strike could go on for another 4 weeks. He was falling behind on bills. Even mortgage payments were late. He was at the bottom. There was only one thing to do, ask Duco for a loan. I was too young to figure out what was happening so I don't know how much my dad borrowed, but it was in the thousands. Dad mentioned once that he used the house as collateral with Duco. What ever the terms were, dad would be able to catch up on his bills.

When we got home Dad sat at the kitchen table with his Christen Bros. Brandy, check book and pen, and then paid off the loan sharks and caught up on all the other legitimate bills. He had money left over for living expenses until the strike ended. Needless to say, he was relieved and stressed at the same time. He started working on that brandy.

That strike was the longest one the Sheet Metal Workers Union would ever have to endure again. They got more money per hour and health benefits. They also would be allowed to invest in a retirement plan. The biggest thing that meant the most was the hourly wage. It was a 2 year contract. This union was maturing into a workforce power house. It put the housing market and commercial building construction to a halt. Heck, it put investors to their knees begging the shop owners to settle. This union grew stronger than ever and it would never look back. Dad was a staunch member too. He wouldn't do anything against union rules. He refused several side jobs involving sheet metal work during the strike.

It was great having that strike in the past, but the workers suffered deeply. The employers were successful in their own way. It was their hope that the men would suffer so much financial hardship that they would beg for the status quo. The men did suffer extreme hardship, but they never gave up.

My dad wasn't the only union man that had to take out a loan. Hundreds of the men were in the same boat financially. They had those damn high interest, high risk loans. Some of them did loose their possessions to these loan sharks. Some filed bankruptcy. This strike hurt a lot of good family men right in the pocketbook. It would take several years to recoup all the money lost during the strike.

During the early and mid 1950's my dad started drinking more and more. The strike took the wind out of him. He was having a tough time paying Duco every month. He realized that his loan terms were just as hard on him as the loan sharks. The shop he was currently working for was not winning any bids for work.

Dad was working less and less hours. The owner was a nice enough guy and did everything he could to keep dad on the payroll. He even had dad take care of his private property by mowing and painting. He still received his union wage and benefit. There would be some shop duties that might add up to a few hours too. It was not a healthy shop. Eventually they closed their doors.

Dad then went to the union hall to enter his name on the list for shops looking for workers. He lucked out on this list. It was a short one. He was hired the same day. I remember that day when he got home. It was a Friday and he was in the mood for a neighborhood party. These get togethers were a weekly thing. There were about 6 households all lined up on the block.

Nearly every Friday or Saturday night they would all gather for a night of drinking, games, flirting, and whatever else tickled their fancy. In the summer they partied outside. In the winter it would be at a house with the basement finished off. Our house was finished off by dad. Mom and dad hosted quite a few parties. On those nights, we kids didn't get much sleep because of the noise and the constant marching of people coming upstairs past our rooms to the bathroom.

The day after the party it was best to stay far away from dad. His hangovers put him in a bad mood. If we got to close to him he would come up with a bunch of chores for me to do. The first thing was to pick up all the party trash and then dust and vacume the basement. The smell of cocktail glasses half full and cigarettes crushed in the ashtrays was enough to make anyone sick. When we were done cleaning the basement we would call dad to inspect our work. Heaven help me if he found a cigarette butt or an empty cocktail glass. If the cleaning didn't meet his standards, we would be made to start over again. This would go on for three to four times until he was finally happy and released us to go play. He sure didn't have to tell me twice to take off.

If a weekend party wasn't going to happen, dad would pack us up and head for Duco and Mables house. When Duco worked for the brewery he was allowed ten cases of mislabeled bottles of beer a week. It cost 1 dollar a case.

Every week Duke would get his quota of ten cases delivered to his house by his truck driver friend, Ole. Duco even gave Ole a spare garage door opener so the beer could be safely put away. I think he would give Ole a couple dollars for this service. If Duco was planning on company coming over during the weekend, he would solicit a brewery non drinker to purchase their quota for him. He would get several extra cases delivered. None of it went to waist. Duco would drink every drop of his quota. So with all that beer, dad found it hard not to go to their house and help Duke drink it. They would usually engage in a conversation or start a game of cards.

Duco didn't like the idle hands of children. He always had a list of chores for us kids to perform. It was always the same when ever we went there. Mow the lawn, pickup twigs, sweep the sidewalk, sweep the garage, do the dishes, and sweep the basement. By the time we got to the basement they were drunk. Our best bet then was to stay in the basement. With the exception of my mom, the rest of them got mean towards us kids. We wouldn't go upstairs for nothing. The farther away we stayed from them, the better. The only person that was safe to go up was Cheryl. Duco and Mable took a high fancy to Cheryl. In their minds she could do no wrong, but those other three brats, humph, they're devils in disguise. So here is the way thing had to go down if we wanted a soda for instance. We would beg Cheryl to go up and ask grandma for some soda pop. Cheryl had the power over us.

She would eventually give in to our request and dash upstairs. The next thing we knew, Cheryl hollered down to us to come up and get our soda. We all went upstairs quiet as mice. In the kitchen nook were three little Dixie cups half full of soda. Cheryl had what was left in the bottle all to her self. It was hardly worth our effort to drink it. When we were done with our soda, back downstairs we went. We would stay there until mom called us up so we could go home. Going home presented a whole new list of fears. We usually argued over the seating arrangements in the car. I always wanted to stay as far away from dad as possible. Some how when he was drunk, I would always piss him off and he would spin around and smack me a few times. I had no idea what I did or said to make him do that, but it happened every time he drank.

The worse part is riding with a very severe drunk driver. I never understand how, after all those years of visiting, we got home safe and without the police stopping us. It boggles my mind even today. It was a 15 mile trip through city streets and also on the freeway. The speed limit on the freeway was 70 MPH and dad would go at least that fast. By the way, mom didn't drive a car until the late 1960's.

Duco and my dad were becoming good drinking buddies. My dad drank fairly heavy before, in fact, he told me of drinking binges the he and some of his soldier buddies endured and survived while in New Caledonia in the middle of the Pacific Ocean. Dad was trained as a chemist and that training helped him in the knowledge in making a home brew from pineapples and coconuts. They would use the juice from the pineapple and add ingredients into a hollowed out coconut. They would fashion a cork for it and let it brew under their bunks. After a couple days with the help of the island heat, they would hear a fizzing coming from their tiny breweries. Soon after the fizzing stopped, the cork would blow off the top signaling the brew was ready to drink. This was a potent drink. Dad said 2 of them would be plenty. They each held about a pint of a pineapple flavored drink.

He had another story to tell me. After Japan surrendered, dad was part of the occupation force in Japan. It was just one big party for him and his buddies. They drank that rice wine, Sake, nearly every day just to pass time. Once on a field trip to a place where the

Sake was cheap and very potent he said he and three buddies were nearly blinded by the stuff. They were driving back to the military compound in their jeep when all of a sudden they noticed a tire rolling past them down the road. They started laughing it off not realizing it was their tire from the rear axle of the jeep. A couple days later he woke up in the hospital all busted up and still hung over from the Sake. The nurses told him the jeep rolled several times tossing the guys around like rag dolls.

Nobody was killed, but everyone was seriously hurt. After she told him that story, he received his every 8 hour Penicillin shot. They needed several days' worth of Penicillin because they landed in a farmer's field. In Japan, they use everything for fertilizer including human waist. They needed the protection from infection and disease. To this day my dad will cry when he sees a needle. So that's when my dad acquired the need for alcohol. He won't even look at Sake or pineapple juice, now its brandy and beer.

Buddies

During the 1950's and early 1960's Duco and my dad were just about attached at the hip. They were drinking more and more every time they were together. By now fishing was there real passion. For Duco, it was his get away. Mable and Duco were fighting every day. Divorce was out of the question for them. Mable didn't want to return to a life without financial stability, and Duco was so tight with money, he would rather have an argument every day than to part with money due to spousal support. He had too much to loose. They were staying together for convenience.

Dad had a different reason to hang with Duke. He owed him money. There were times when his monthly budget would be a bit tight and by drinking with Duco and being his friend, sometimes Duco would let him slide with a payment. The relationship worked for both of them. Plus the fact they really had fun together. At least the male bonding they had wasn't anything like the bonding Duco had back in 1933.

It started out in the early 1950's with day trips to Mille Lac Lake in central Minnesota. They would take Duco's Cadillac early Saturday morning and drive the 110 miles north to the lake. If a bar happened to be open along the way, they would stop for a few drinks.

They would have a favorite resort where they would rent time on the resorts launch. The launch would usually leave the dock at 10:00 am and take a group out to the hot spots on a four hour trip. The launch always had beer and set ups for sale. The two men would certainty buy their share of beer. The launch captain knew where the fishermen could catch their limit of Walleye and the guys usually would limit out. At about 2:00 PM the launch returns to the dock. Dad and Duke would go into the resort for a hamburger and then jump in the car for a bit of bar hoping.

They would hit bars around the lake until around 4:00 pm and then head south for the 110 mile trip home. Of coarse they would have to stop along the way for a few drinks. When they arrived back home they would clean the fish they caught and divide the fillets evenly. On Monday we would have a Walleye supper. You haven't had a good fish until you've had fresh Walleye. These trips went on for a few years. It was around 1955 that Duco and dad built a winter fish house. It was 8 foot by 10 foot in size. It had a double sized bed for sleeping and a wood burning stove. They built it so it was collapsible.

They could haul it on a small trailer and set it up anywhere they wished. They started out on Lake Minnetonka. It's a large lake in the western area of the metropolitan area.

This is when they started bringing me along on weekend fishing trips. Lake Minnetonka was close to home and the fish house was an experiment for the two some. We didn't catch fish like we really wanted; they were usually small Northern Pike that we released. Every now and then we would catch a small Walleye. Again, they were too small to keep. The fish house was doing what they expected, it kept us warm. As I remember we fished that lake for only 2 seasons.

We just couldn't get the fish we wanted. They decided to build a house a bit bigger. It would be an 8 foot by 12 foot. This time dad used his employers' delivery truck to haul the house to Mille Lac Lake. It was just him and I that took off on a Friday afternoon to Portside Resort. We went up a day earlier than Duco. Work was a bit slow for dad, so he decided to take half the day off. When we arrived at the resort, the owner greeted us and welcomed us as new customers. I guess a little explanation is due here on these resort operations during the winter.

On Mille Lacs during the winter fishing season, resorts have beefed up 4 wheel drive pickup trucks fitted with 10 foot wide V-plows. These trucks had extra axel springs to support a plow and a tow truck like boom in the bed of the truck. This boom aided the truck with chains that hooked to houses. It when attached properly it put more weight on the real axle and also pulled the back of the truck down hard on the rear tires for added traction. It also would break the house skids loose from the ice. Then they could pull the fish house anywhere. These trucks would run 18 hours a day. They would have constant breakdowns. Transmissions were usually the biggest problem.

The resort would test the ice thickness every day until it reached 12 – 14 inches thick. Then the ice would support the weight of the plow trucks. Now the resorts would start plowing roads on the lake to various reefs and deeper water holes. When the roads were plowed, they would start hooking up to their rental fish houses, (they varied in size), and pulled them out on the lake. Once they had all their rental houses out on the lake they would start pulling private houses out. Usually the house owner would have scouted out a place to park his house. It would then be the resorts duty to keep a road plowed to that house so the customer can drive to it. Some of the average sized resorts could have up to 400 – 500 private houses plus their rentals. This was big business and resort owners treated their customers very well.

Dad and I arrived at the resort and the resort owner greeted us, he offered us a rental to use overnight until Duco arrived to help set up our fish house. Setting it up was a bit more than we could handle. We took the owner up on his offer. He led the way out onto the lake to the rental we would stay in overnight. Well, this house was small to say the least. It had a fuel oil burning stove and two fish holes drilled out. I think it was a 6 foot by 8 foot. It had two wooden chairs and that was all. Oh well, we baited two lines and dropped them in the lake. We had some sandwiches and of coarse dad had his beer and brandy and I had a soda.

We were set for the night. I'll be darned; the walleye started biting at sundown. We couldn't pull them out fast enough. They were all good sized keepers too. What a blast! We lit our lantern and had to actually stop fishing to count them. We had our limit! We didn't fish anymore that night. We just sat and talked about how much fun we had. It was a special moment for us. It was really late and we were both getting sleepy. We had a news paper with us and we spread it on the floor. We lay on the floor and took turns sleeping next to the stove all night. If we slept for an hour, I'd be surprised. When the sun came up Duco had just pulled up to the house. He couldn't believe our luck. He said, "Let's set our house up right here!" It took about an hour to build it up and get the stove fired up.

That bed was a welcome sight and I jumped into the covers. Darn, that bed was cold! I forgot that it sat in the truck all night in 10 degree weather. It wasn't warmed up yet. Duco brought a bunch of groceries and home left over meals. The house was completely self contained with utilities. That morning he made salt pork and eggs on the wood burning stove. Best breakfast I ever had. This was the beginning of weekend trips that would eventually turn into nightmares for me and sometimes my sisters. The only good thing about these winter weekends, they ended every February 14th when the Walleye season ended until May.

As the weekends went by the boys were starting to drink more and more. They found friends within the resorts clientele that also liked to drink. The more they drank, the more they ignored us kids. In fact, it was getting so bad the word got back to mom and she wouldn't let my sisters go there anymore. It wasn't the right atmosphere for girls. It was ok for a ten year old boy though. When it came right down to it, Duco and I never did see eye to eye with each other. He was a mean SOB when he drank. He was down right abusive too.

It was my chore to wash the dishes in the fish house. First of all, we never used paper plates and we had only one large pot to boil lake water. There was a system to cleaning up the dishes. Here's how it went.

In the bottom of the huge pot I would place a plate upside down. Then I would add lake water and dish soap and then all the dirty dishes and pans on top of the upside down plate. This was done in the evening after supper. This pot would sit on the stove all night. At about 2:00 am the water started to heat up and the plate would percolate a big bubble. It would do this faster as the water got hotter. It was an automatic dishwasher. By morning I would use tongs and retrieve the dishes and place them on the table. Some may have needed a little touch up. I would dump the water outside and then rinse the pot with lake water. I would then put the dishes back in the pot, put a fair amount of water in it, turn up the heat and wait for the water to boil. Usually in 15 minutes. Then I could take the dishes out with the tongs and dry them and put them away.

This was done twice a weekend. What sometimes made this so darn hard was the fact that Duco never cooked a meal sober. He always burned food in the pans. They were a chore by themselves to clean. Duco wanted those pans so clean; he could use them as a mirror. He meant it too.

Both of those guys were heavy smokers. It's a wonder I didn't get a lung disease from all that second hand smoke. The inside of the house was blue with smoke all day and most of the night. Duco also made sure they had plenty of beer to drink. The trunk of his Cadillac was full of cases of Grain Belt. We always rode to the lake in the Cadillac. I think it was an ego booster for Duco to use the Cadillac.

The two some also liked to drink brandy. When they had friends visit them in the house Duco liked to make them highballs. His favorite was brandy and 7up. Soon enough his friends were drunk and the bottle was empty. Duco would hand me the bottle and give me two choices. 1. Walk to other fish houses and ask for a booze donation. Go house to house until the bottle was full. 2. Walk to shore and tell the owner to replace the bottle and put the price on a tab. A lot of this decision was based on two things. 1. How cold is it outside? 2. How far was shore? We normally placed the house 2 – 3 miles out from shore. More often than not, I would be knocking on doors. I would bring back the most ungodly mixture of booze you can imagine. These knot heads drank it! I can't begin to tell you just how drunk these guys would get. They couldn't even talk. To this day I'm surprised they didn't die from alcohol poisoning. Who knows what was in that bottle?

This is my beginning with those two. Things between Duco and me would get worse. Dad would stand by. He didn't want Duco mad at him. He knew Duco held a second mortgage on the house. I would be his sacrificial Lamb.

Fish Houses

After I was discharged from the Army dad and I went into a kind of partnership with fish houses. After I was introduced to his Mille Lacs toys I was hooked. We used that first house he built for several years. After noticing other fishermen building bigger house we decided to build a 10 foot by 14 foot house. Dad sold the first house to his friend George.

That fall when the weather was cooler and we hunted for Partridge we started on our bigger house. We would work on the house at sun up until about an hour before sundown. Then we would go into the woods and hunt birds until dark. When we were done hunting we would jump into the saloon for supper and then drink until closing time. We would stay in Duke's mobile home at night.

When the house was finished it would be one of the most modern houses on the lake. It was totally contained with everything you would expect in a lake cabin. We ran electrical power with 12 volt car batteries. It had 4 fish holes, one in every corner. Two twin sized beds, one each end. It had a three burner cook top with oven. We installed an extra large TV antenna for our color television, and many other luxuries. It was warm and cozy. My uncle liked it so much he bought it for the following season.

Dad and I went back to the drawing board and designed a 10 foot by 16 foot house. Again we worked on it in the fall for the same reasons. We used lighter material in this house with better insulation. Everything remained the same. We put it out of the ice and we had an excellent fishing season. We met a fellow name Bill during a night of partying at the resort. He liked our fish house and wanted to by it. Dad and I had plenty to drink that night but we weren't too crazy about selling the house. Dad shot a price at Bill that he hoped would back him away. It didn't work. Bill wrote a check for the house right then and there. That house was sold.

Back to the drawing board we went. We will build another 10 foot by 16 foot house. This time we had a steel floor frame and skids made up for it. The carriage of this house was indestructible. The floor plan was the same but the interior walls had upgraded paneling with a brick design mixed with a light color. It was a brighter interior. You may have guessed it, we got two years out of it and someone offered a price we couldn't refuse. It sold for over $3500.00 in 1985. We designed one more house. We scaled this one down a bit. It was a 10 foot by 14 foot house. An extra feature was a garden window. We just got one year from this one before it was sold too.

By now we were getting burned out on building houses. Dad bought a small piece of property across the highway from the lake during an auction. It was an underdeveloped area with several wooded lots up for a walk around auction. We heard about it in a saloon near there. We were fairly loaded with beer and needed the walk so we went to the walk around. Neither of us walked very straight. As we stopped at one corner lot the auctioneer was babbling off the prices and every once in a while he point our way. This went on for a couple minutes and he pointed our way and said sold. Sold? I didn't raise my hand, why is he pointing my way? I looked at my dad and he was reaching for his checkbook. He just bought that corner lot! Oh boy! Does he have a lot of explaining when he gets home? I thought that we had one beer too many. He swore he knew what he was doing.

That lot turned out to be one big tree removing project. I'll bet he took out 75 trees. We found an old 12 foot by 64 foot repo mobile home and placed it on the lot. It took as much work as the lot. After a couple years we had our party house. We bought an old fish house for $250.00 and used that in the winter season for fishing. At night we stayed in the mobile home. We soon got tired of winter fishing. The last year we used that old house; I used my truck and pulled it off the lake to the lot. From then on it became a storage shed. That ended our winter fishing.

It was just the beginning of weekend party's at the mobile home. We fixed it up to a point where it looked new. We put on a deck and new wood paneled exterior. New carpet and we scrubbed the place hospital clean. The air conditioning was unique. Dad replaced a freezing unit at a Dairy Queen. He asked his boss if he could keep the old freezer unit and his boss said it was fine with him. We put that 1000 pound unit and mounted it to a platform then we placed it in the back of the trailer. Dad's friend and work supervisor Doug was also an air-conditioning service technician. He came up to the trailer one day and wired it up. He got the thing running. Man, was that trailer cold! We had refrigeration! Not air conditioning.

The River Lot

Around 1959 Duco purchased a 28 foot Owens cabin cruiser. It was a wooden cruiser with a full galley and head with shower. It had a Chevy six cylinder engine with a fixed shaft driven prop. He kept the cruiser at Sobota Marine near Fort Snelling along the Minnesota River. Duco was doing alright for himself. Nice big house, new Cadillac, a sporty 1959 MG Sportster, and a cabin cruiser. Not bad for an electrician. That wouldn't be all.

He traded his MG Sportster in on a piece of property that sat along the Minnesota River in Lilidale, Minnesota. It was located about three miles down river from Fort Snelling. The lot its self was 2 acres with a under developed yard with junky looking grass. It had a caped basement foundation that was meant to support a house. Next to the foundation was an oversized garage with a second floor. This would be Duco's get away from Mable for a few years.

The first thing he did was enlist dad in helping the development of the lot. Duco made an agreement with dad. He would let him work off his debt by helping him build a dock and several out buildings. Between the two men, dad was by far the brighter of the two when it came to constructing buildings. Duco knew electricity, but only within the confines of the brewery. Dad worked with all the trades building houses. He learned from the other tradesmen and they learned from him. It was a good deal Duco offered him.

They would get together on Wednesday, Saturday and Sunday. Wednesday was usually just for a couple hours to plan for the next weekend. It gave Duco time to purchase the items needed for the weekend work.

The first order of business was to have me clean the garage. Not just clean it, he wanted it scoured. He would install a well and have the garage fit with plumbing and fixtures, (toilet), and a cooking stove. Dad installed a heating system. The garage was transformed into a home complete with a work shop.

My next chore was to mow that damn lawn every week, one and a half acres of bumpy tough grass and weeds. No shade trees to take a bit of shelter under, just 2 solid acres of crappy grass. It took three hours every weekend to mow that lawn. Guess what I got out of it. Nothing! When I was done mowing I had another chore Duco made me do. He had a truck load of old lumber delivered.

He wanted the nails pulled out, straightened and saved. I was 12 – 13 year old and small for my age. There can't be anything more challenging then pulling screw type nails out of oak wood.

I had more sprains in my arms and shoulder than I can count. Then try to hold one of those nails down and hit it with a hammer to make it straight. I bled a lot for a person I didn't like.

Duco didn't like paying the slip fee at the marina for his cruiser. The first order of business was to build a huge slip for the boat. Got to give them credit for this one, the dock would be an accomplishment beyond his original dreams. The 150 foot shoreline had a steep 15 foot bank down to the water. They built stairs to reach the water. At the waters edge there was about 8 feet of sandy shoreline. The bank had several truckloads of limestone dumped on it to prevent erosion. The limestone came from a torn down building. Duco got these loads delivered free.

The next thing he did was to have a telephone pole drove into the river about 15 feet from the shores edge. It was pounded down about 15 feet by professionals with a barge. Then the guys built the floating dock. It was fastened around the pole in an "A" frame fashion. The dock was built with two sides extending from the "A" frame about 30 feet on both sides. It was built on top of 55 gallon drums that Duco received from the brewery. He had the brewery shop weld the drums top and bottom to seal them.

When they built the frame work for the dock, all those nails came into play. Duco cut and placed the planks in place. He called me to him and said he wanted me to get a hammer and the nails I straightened and go down and nail down the planks.

This would be a hard job. Oak isn't easy to drive nails through. It's a very hard wood. Those darn nails were going to bend over too. I gathered up the nails and a hammer and walked down the stairs to the dock. As I was walking down I heard Duco call for my dad to watch something. I looked back up and saw them watching me. I found out why after I got on the dock. I took about two steps and a board came up and slapped me in the face. I went down like a tree. I was out cold.

I came to in a few seconds and the first thing I noticed was all the blood around my head. The second thing I noticed was those two drunks laughing their heads off. Duco set me up on this. Dad finally came down to help me up. I was groggy and bleeding from the nose and mouth.

I had one huge lump on my forehead too. Dad reached into his pocket and dragged out his snot filled handkerchief and put it against my bleeding face. He had to carry me upstairs to the garage and finally use water and towel to stop the bleeding. I was done working for the day. I had a blinding headache. From that day on they called me the "Dumb Kid". It was my fault that the board hit me according to them. The next day we went back and I still had to nail the deck down. This time I was testing every step.

When these two guys got drunk I was their little prankster child. I was the butt of all their sick jokes. For instance, after a days' work, Duco and dad would take the cruiser out for a ride. I never wanted to go because I knew what was in store for me. Once out on the river and cruising they thought it was great sport to grab me, tip me upside down and grab me by the ankles and then hang me over the side and threaten to let go. I couldn't swim! They were drunk and I wasn't so sure about their grip. They thought this was funny. I didn't.

On top of the chores that I was supposed to do, I also had my school homework along with me. I could never get to it and my grades suffered. That became a double edged sword. I had to do those chores when I went to the lot. I also had a lawn to mow at home that was just as big. Dad always had chores for me to do at home too. I was becoming a failure in school. I couldn't get homework done because I was loaded with chores and all the chores just plain wore me out. I would fall to sleep in school. When report cards came out my grades were bad. Dad would see them and beat the hell out of me and then accuse me of being stupid and lazy.

He had become Duco! They would never believe that I was saturated with chores. If I didn't do the chores, it was another beating. There was nothing I could do. I was in a vicious trap. My salvation was my other set of grandparents.

Clyde and Irene were my dad's mom and step dad. They knew I was being abused and did all they could to rescue me. They would take me away from home to live with them for extended periods of time. Grandma Irene would jump all over my dad if she saw bruising on me, and she sometimes did. They knew the history behind Duco and Mable and they never associated with them. They didn't like the fact that dad would allow Duco to make me do those chores. They saved my butt several times like that. I did spend a lot of time with Clyde and Irene and they were the safest moments in my life.

There was a problem though. I eventually had to go home. It took about 2 days for dad to steam up.

Then he would have a few shots of brandy and then blow up and chase me downstairs. I got him in trouble with his mother and I was going to pay! When he got done with me I couldn't look at him for days. I wanted out of that house but I had nowhere to go. At this time my mother was going through severe depression stemming from her childhood. She couldn't help me, she couldn't help herself. I was doomed to live with abuse until I was big enough to fight back.

Duco developed the property with a dock for his cruiser, several out buildings, a chicken coupe, a duck pond and shelter, and a pig pen for 2 pigs. They would grow and end up in our freezers. The boys built their little empire.

In 1965 the Minnesota River reached a record breaking flood level. It wiped out everything except the garage on the lot. Fortunately, the animals were moved to a farm and the cruiser was dry docked high and dry. Duco was able to retrieve all his power equipment before the flood peaked. The foundation was nearly destroyed along with the dock. The dock ended up downriver several miles. This was the end of the river lot. Duco would sell this at a profit, of course.

He kept the cruiser for a while longer and kept it docked at Sabota's. His next move would surprise us all. In the mean time he would be spending time at home with Mable. They were going to torment each other until Duco finally figured out a way to stay away from home for weeks at a time. Retirement has a lot to do with his plans.

One other thing, during 1964 and 1965, I had a growth spurt that put me over 6 feet. I was built fairly well in proportion. My size now was a bit intimidating to Duke. I now remember from his prison time, he would never challenge anyone his size or bigger. He was a big man with a gun in his hand, but he wasn't so big with out it.

In prison he had Cleon and Walter to back him. Those two were always prepared for a fight. Both of them had many survival fights when they served time in the St. Cloud prison. Stillwater wasn't any different. Just as soon as you pick out the inmate that thinks he's the toughest, you beat the hell out of him to establish your rank among the rest of the population. Cleon and Walter worked well together establishing this ranking. Duco was ranked with them by default.

During the years of 1964 and 1965 the river lot was a place for me to take my friends and raise a little hell. There were the four of us that had motorcycles and we would go to the lot with our girl friends for a bit of privacy. Nothing sexual mind you, we were all brought up with some strict values. We went to the lot to just be kids. We got to know a few of the neighbor kids and chummed around with them.

Duco had no problem with us being there. By then his interest in the place was winding down. I think even before the flood he was thinking about selling the lot. He waited a year to long. I had my own key to the garage and we would kind of refer to the place as our club house. I was at an age and size where Duco gave me a few liberties.

We used to be professional wrestling fans. On Saturday Vern Gagne, a local wrestling czar, put on a wrestling TV show at 6:00 pm. This show was a tease for the main events that would take place later that night at the Minneapolis Auditorium. Our families attended quite a few of the main events.

One Saturday there was some kind of grudge match going to happen at the main event. It was good vs. evil that couldn't be missed. I asked dad if he wanted to go. He didn't but suggested I ask Duke. I called Duco and asked him. He said yes, he wanted to go. I said I was on my way to his house and hung up. I jumped on my Harley Davidson 125 Sportster and headed to Minneapolis. 20 minutes later I arrived at Dukes house and he was in the open garage waiting for me. So I drove into the garage to park the bike and jump into the Caddy. To my surprise, Duco wanted to ride on the back of the bike to the auditorium. Wow! OK! He jumped on the back and away we went. I couldn't believe this. He was laughing all the way. I never heard him laugh before. This was a special moment that I experienced for the first time with him.

When I got home later that night, I told dad about it. He was shocked. He said that maybe Duco sees you now as an adult. Must be true, Duco's meanness towards me stopped in 1965. I was a senior in school and would graduate next spring. We all knew once I graduated, I was a prime candidate for the military draft. That day was approaching way to fast. I wasn't going to let the draft board get me!

In Uniform

During the river lot days and the ice fishing days I never saw much of Mable. My time was spent with the men. The times I did spend with her were holidays. No matter how much Duco disliked kids, he was at his best when he hosted Thanksgiving, Easter, and Christmas Eve. Mable was a darn good cook. The dinning room table was a very pretty picture to behold. They had the finest china and silverware. They used crystal glasses and very nice looking candle holders with a bright burning candle and to bring out the colors, she always displayed a bunch of seasonal flowers. The turkey was the center piece and every year pictures had to be taken. Duco would always be the one to carve the turkey, and he did that at the table. One by one he would ask if the person wanted white or dark meat. He would slice their order and place it on their plate. These times were the only times that we kids could be kids. We were allowed to play and not perform chores. We didn't even have to help with dishes.

There were times when mom had to go into the hospital for one reason or another. Her depression was a major reason for a few admissions. On at least 2 occasions she needed shock treatments.

They didn't help her much. The other few times in the hospital were for female problems that needed surgeries and focused counseling.

I would say that ¾ of the times when mom was in the hospital I would stay with Clyde and Irene. The other times I stayed with Mable and Duco. These were the times when I was treated as an inconvenience. Now that I look back on the way Mable acted toward me, I think she looked at me the same way she looked at her daughter Darlos. Mavis was treated like princes. I believe she was treated better because she was born while Mable was married to Julian Peterson. She was a legitimate child born from a married couple. Darlos, on the other hand, was born from Mable's prostitution and more than likely from a person she needed to protect. My mother constantly asked Mable who her father was. It was always the same answer, "It's not important for you to know".

Mable held that secret until her last breath. I really mean her last breath. When she was on her death bed she became conscience for a few moments. Mother was next to her and asked her one more time who her father was. Mable's dieing gasp was the same answer she always gave, "It's not important for you to know". Then she died. I was in the room and I couldn't believe the cruelty she expressed to the very end.

Mable called Darlos her unwanted child. She called her that all her life. Whenever they had an argument, Mable would end it by stating she was an unwanted one and arguing with you means nothing. Mavis would always win the arguments with her mom. The very few times they argued, Mable would cave in and tell Mavis, "I think you know best". The favoritism Mable had towards Mavis was sickening. Mable coddled her like an egg. What ever Mavis needed, be it emotionally or financially, Mable saw to it and gave her what she needed.

Strange as it may be, Dad would protect mom to the end. Neither Duco nor Mable dared pick on mom while he was around. He would stand up to them when it came to her. He knew how Mable treated her all her life. If he needed to pull out their past and use it against them, he would do it. They hurt her enough.

Here is my take why they didn't like me. My parents were married in January, late January at that. I was born August 5th. The arithmetic says I was born more than a month early, but my birth certificate said I was a full term baby. Now using the word illegitimate is a bit tough to use when I challenged mom. I said no matter how it worked out, I'm here and I have a mom and dad. No problem for me.

Duco held the papers on the loan. Mable had no control or say how the money Duco earned was spent. Duco gave her a $40.00 allowance every week. That was for groceries and any personal items she needed.

In my senior year, I worked at Montgomery Wards in South Town Mall in Bloomington. I liked working there. I worked in the warehouse and I also drove the delivery truck for home deliveries of appliances. I was making darn good money for a kid. I liked it so much I quit my English class just so I could get an extra hour of work. I didn't mind going to summer school. They mailed my diploma a couple weeks later.

My mother wasn't happy about me dropping out of the hour class. What worried her most is what Mable would think. I put my cards on the table that day. I told mom exactly what I thought of school and that witch Mable. I didn't know about her criminal record yet, but I told mom there was something wrong with that woman. The way she treats you and other people is criminal. I don't give a damn what she thinks. I felt better. I think mom felt better hearing that from me. The subject never came up again.

I worked hard and long hours that summer. I was finished with school and I was just waiting for my number to come up with the draft board. My friends were all finding doctors to write draft exemptions. They all got them.

There were doctors back then that would do that for a price. It pissed me off that my friends would cheat their way out of the draft. I may have been only 18 years old, but I had quite a bit of patriotism in my heart and a high sense of duty. I liked the country I lived in. Freedom, what a great way of life, and that's all the people in Viet Nam wanted. I understood that. Heck with it, I enlisted in the Army. I felt safer in the Army than at home anyway. I entered the Army October 25, 1966 and had my basic training at El Paso, Texas. From there I went to Ft. Huachuca, Arizona for advanced truck driver training. Then my first duty station was at the Gary, Indiana Nike Missile Headquarters.

While in Gary I was the Chaplains assistant and driver. For a year we were assigned to deliver NOK's,(next of kin), notices to the survivors of our soldiers killed in Viet Nam or in the area we covered. We were the heartbreak Army car that showed up in the driveway like what you would see at a movie. It should be known that soldiers also died state side from accidents, disease, sometimes suicide and even homicide. Our area covered the greater Chicago area, southeastern Wisconsin, and northern Indiana.

We assigned funeral homes for the burial. Our duty was to receive the body at the airport and escort it to the funeral home. We also performed an inspection of the funeral directors work to make sure the body was presented according to military directives. Military funerals have very strict rules and regulations when it came to honoring a fallen soldier. I don't think the military had a more depressing job than what we did. The balance of my service was spent in Germany. I had the full time duty being the night charge of quarters. Charge of quarters was the company night supervisor. It was my duty to keep law and order in the company compound. I also escorted payroll personnel to their duty places and guarded them and the money while the soldiers were being paid. This was always a bit harrowing considering the officer carrying the money had 10's of thousands of dollars on him at the same time every month. We always travelled the same route at the same time every month. I often wondered if anyone ever timed us and planned a robbery.

I had an assistant called a "runner" and we were the two people in charge of the night operations of the company. We worked three nights in a row and then we were off four nights. We also had a class "A" passes. It meant no restrictions. We could live off post and we did.

Going back to my time spent in Gary, it was just a nine hour drive back to Minneapolis. I had my car with me in Gary. Every now and then I would take a weekend plus a two day pass and go back home for 4 days.

By now Duco had carried out his new plan. He sold the cruiser and bought a lot and a mobile home in Mille Lac Lake. He spent just about all his spare cash on this lake home. The mobile home was an extra insulated special winterized home with two bedrooms and a fireplace. He had a well put in a heated man sized pit in the middle of his concrete driveway. He built an extra long double wide concrete and block garage, Half the garage had his 16 foot fishing boat sitting on a ramp that extended down to the water. He had an electric winch to move it up and down the ramp. The other half of the garage housed his Caddy and a work shop with his favorite power tools. His yard was professionally landscaped. He had one of the most decent homes on that side of the lake.

He was retired. He would stay at the lake for weeks on end. He would go home once in a while to collect his retirement checks and his social security check. He would pay his bills and then head back to the lake.

Mable was home alone for weeks on end. It was fine for the first few months, but soon the house was starting to close in on her. She had to take care of the inside and outside. Duco wasn't around to mow the lawn so it was up to her. She made up her mind about this house. It had to be sold and she wanted an apartment now. She wouldn't have to mow a lawn.

The next time Duco came home they talked about selling the house. Mable made her point that the lawn work was to hard on her. They also said that all the grandchildren have grown and the family wasn't getting together anymore for the holidays. They didn't need this big house anymore. They mutually agreed to sell and move into an apartment.

Duco sold the house to a fine couple on a contract for deed. He took a sizable down payment and set monthly payments with 8% interest and had a final balloon payment set for sometime in the early 1970's. It was a great deal for everyone. Mable and Duco moved into an apartment with one bedroom along Minnehaha Avenue in south Minneapolis.

Duco did something that Mable didn't know about. He took the apartment and also the caretakers duties. He would get a sizable discount on the rent. The building was small so vacuuming the halls wouldn't take long. They didn't need to mow. The owner had a service for that. All they had to do was the hallway once a day, and clean vacated apartments for newcomers and collect the rent from the other seven tenants. Simple duties, he thought for a discount, Mable can take care of things here.

I'm glad I was in Gary when that happened. When Mable found out that she would be home alone and taking care of an apartment building, you could nearly see the mushroom cloud from Gary. Dad said that the argument went on for a week non stop.

He said Mable had to call him several times because Duco had threatened her life and appeared to mean it. If fact one time when dad arrived he was sitting on her with a knife in his hand. Dad talked him down and took away the knife.

So the house was sold and they had moved into the apartment. Duco went to the lake. He would stay for a month. His funds were running low and he didn't want to go home. He patronized Liberty Beach Resort. Nearly every day he would go there for a few beers and conversation. He was so well liked in the place; the owners asked him if he wanted to bar tend part time. He said he would and it sounded like fun. Every afternoon he would bar tend. He was a great story teller. To the resort owner's surprise, more and more people were showing up when Duco was the bartender. Duco was having a blast. He would bar tend and pour himself a few beers, until about 6:00 pm, go home and have supper, then put the boat in the lake for a couple hours of fishing. On weekends dad would join him and stay in the second bedroom. For two days they would drink and fish. On Saturday night they would go to Liberty Beach and party with the crowd.

On some of my four day passes I would go up to the lake and join them. After I enlisted in the Army, Duco had a whole new respect for me. He actually was treating me like a grandson. We were doing things together. We would fish, play cards, go to the bar at Liberty, visit some of his friends and the thing we enjoyed most was cooking a boiled dinner together. We had the same taste when it came to the ingredients.

One time we got a pot of boiled dinner going and then sat down for a few card games and beer. We got carried away with the beer and forgot about the boiled dinner on the stove. We burned up a great supper! We went to the bar and had hamburgers and beer. We had far too many beers to go fishing that night so the three of us stayed in the bar until the Saturday night band arrived.

All night long we sat at a table drinking beer and singing songs along with the band. It was as memorable night as the one where we went to the wrestling matches on my motorcycle. This was the last I would see Duco healthy. Two weeks later I went to Germany for two years.

Mom was the letter writer and so was Grandma Irene. I never received anything from Mable. Not even a Christmas card. That woman really didn't like me. Anyway, mom would keep me current on family business. I don't recall many letters referring to Mable and Duco until I was about to come home. I was to be discharged October 5, 1969.

I left Frankfort, Germany and was in a plane heading for Fort Dix, New Jersey on October 4th. Then on the 5th I went through all the red tape the Army tossed at me for my honorable discharge. I was finally on a plane to Minneapolis that evening. Once we landed I grabbed my duffle bag and caught a taxi home. They didn't know I was coming. When I got home I just walked right in and said, "I'm home!" What a great feeling that was.

Everyone was in the living room watching television and talking with Marsha. I don't know how that happened, but Marsha was my sweetheart before I went to Germany. Out of fairness to both of us, we split up when I left. I was really surprised she was there and it was truly coincidence. Nobody knew for sure what day I'd be home. We all stayed up until mid night and then called it a night. The next day my mom would tell me a story that would take my breath away.

Now You Tell Me

I was home and it felt good. I had no idea what I was going to do for a job, but I wasn't worried about it. When I was discharged I received a fair amount of money. It was enough to last for a few months. The next morning I woke up and had coffee with dad. We chatted until he had to leave for work. He tossed me the keys to my car and said I might want to wash it. He used it for work during my two years in Germany. We walked out the door together. He got into his car and left for work while I inspected my car. What a mess! He used it on muddy job sites and he carried all his dirty tools in it. It had gravel in the grill! He never washed it. I could never get my car clean. A short time later I bought a new car. I would never let my dad use my car again for any reason.

I guess the first thing I did the next day was to catch up with all my friends to see how they spent the last three years. One of my friends actually joined the Army and ended up in Viet Nam. The poor guy was nearly torn to pieces by a hand grenade tossed into his tent. He wore a metal plate in his head and wasn't quite the same. I respected him for serving and he didn't deserve what happened to him. For that matter, none of the guys deserved what happened to them. The battle field injured is the most honorable men in my mind. My other two friends bought a doctor that wrote physical disabilities for them and that took them off the draft list. I lost a lot of respect them.

My grandma Irene passed away six months before I came home. My second day home would be going to Clyde's house and then to her grave site. It would be hard to see Clyde all by himself.

Mom told me she would really like a talk with me about some serious family business. I said, "sure, how about now?" It was about 7:00 pm and mom did what she always did when we had to talk, she warmed up some milk and made a couple cups of Ovaltine. Now I new she had something very serious to talk about.

She started out by saying Duco has cancer of the pancreas. It was terminal and he had about 5 months to live. He was at the apartment now and he wants to die there. She said he is still mobile around the home but can't drive anymore. He is on extremely powerful pain medications. Mable is taking good care of him. They are trying so hard not to argue so he doesn't get upset and nauseated. He throws up a lot of blood when he gets upset. So she tries her best to keep him calm. Dad is taking care of the lake home. Duco requested him to do that. Duco told him to use it when ever he wants. There is a young man and his wife that helped Mable with the building. They also washed the Caddy once a week. Duco wants it that way. He's always so fussy on his appearance, and that includes the Caddy. Mom requested that I go see him. He asks about me often. He was proud of me when I enlisted and he always mentioned me to his friends. He wants to see me. I would go there tomorrow.

Mom made another round of Ovaltine. I kind of figured something big was coming. This time she looked at me with tears in her eyes.

I could see words were hard to get out. That's when she told me that Duco and Mable were convicted felons and they both served time in prison. This was brought up years ago. At that time we weren't told too many details. This time she explained everything to me. That is, everything that she knew. It took a while for her to get it all out in the open. It was the third round of Ovaltine that shook me to the core. That's when the story about her Uncle Fred and the "John's" that Mable entertained came out with a stream of tears. She told me how her mother always said she was unwanted and wouldn't divulge her real fathers' name. Mom gave me her whole story. It was way past midnight before she could take a long cleansing breath. The whole story as she remembered it was out. She said my sisters already were told. She pleaded with me not to let Mable and Duco know that I found out what they really are. I said it's going to be hard to even look at them the same way anymore. I won't let on about this, but I never liked them before, and that feeling is even deeper now. I was speechless.

The next day I went to see Duco. It was the longest drive that I could remember. The thoughts of my mothers' abuse went through my mind over and over. I tried to imagine how tortured she was as a toddler. How horrified she must have been when her own mother allowed strangers to touch her. What kind of person would hold back information about a question of genealogy and heritage? I can only picture my grandmother as a monster that lurks in the minds of normal people. Only a monster could commit such evil crimes against a child. It all makes sense to me now. I understood why she behaved the way she did with me. That woman has larceny in her heart and it will never go away. She is mean to her core and nothing or nobody will ever change her. Even after serving her one year in prison she returned to prostitution.

She tried to take money away from a family's child support that had Duco's blood line. She wanted Duco to give her spousal support while she was prostituting herself and also living with different men at different times. She was using her daughter as enhancement for her customer sexual needs. She was the catalyst that would ignite the fire in the minds of the gang that would set them out on their crime sprees.

She knew how to use a hand gun and she more than likely was one of the shooters that tried to kill Oscar that night in Benson. Mable was capable of anything. Even at this point in time as Duco waits to die, she can't be trusted. I will never look at her as a grandmother again. I will research every aspect of their lives. I will dig out the truth and some day I will tell the world how evil walks among us without us knowing it. If she was the catalyst for the crime sprees as I suspect, she can take the blame for her brother Nobles death. Without her cheering the gang on to more robberies, they never would have stopped in Benson. Nobel would maybe still be alive.

I finally arrived at their apartment. I parked at the front of the building and just sat there for a while. I saw Mable looking out at me from her picture window. I wondered what she was thinking. Maybe she was wondering what I was thinking. I wanted to throw up. After a few minutes I got out of the car and walked up to the door and rang the bell. Grandma, being a smart ass asked, "Who is it?" I said, you were just looking at me, it's Ken!" The door buzzed and I walked in and then up a few stairs to their apartment. Grandma had the door open and we said hi to each other. She stated that Duco was in the kitchen. I walked past grandma towards the kitchen and there sat Duco, looking out the kitchen window. Duco looked up at me and said, "Welcome home boy. Beer is in the fridge, go ahead and grab one."

I looked at Duco. He was sitting at the kitchen table with a cup of coffee and starring out the window at some birds. He didn't look that much worse for the wear. He was wearing his usual kaki trousers and a white t-shirt. His face looked a bit drawn in but other than that it being unshaven for a couple days he looked alright. He didn't look anything like what I pictured a person would look like dying from cancer. I grabbed a beer and sat down at the table. I looked at him and wanted to say something but the words just couldn't come out. He looked at me with a smile and said he was glad I was home safe. He said he thought about me everyday and all his friends at the lake were wishing me well too. He proceeded to tell me some stories about his lake episodes. They were interesting stories so I sat and listened. After about a half hour I could see he was getting tired. Mable said he should go lay down for a while now. I got up to help him get up.

It was then I noticed the devastation the cancer has caused. There was nothing to him. His huge 6 foot 200 pound frame was gone. He was so skinny I was afraid I'd break a bone lifting him. Every move he made was labored and painful. I more or less carried him to bed. Mable followed me with his pain medication. I think he was taking a powerful strength of Dilaudid. She gave him two heaping table spoons of the pain medication and not even a minute latter he fell to sleep. He looked at peace.

I went out and sat on the couch and asked Mable how this all came about. She mentioned that three years ago he went into the hospital get his yearly physical. Just so you all know, Duco took a week of from work with pay and checked into the hospital for a physical. His good friend Dr. Vick would conduct this physical. Duco had a private room with television, a couch, refrigerator stocked with Grain Belt beer, cheese, summer sausage, olive, pickles, and herring. He would also have crackers and potato chips at the ready. This was his idea of a physical. He paid out of his own pocket for this week.

On this physical the x-rays showed a spot on Duco's lung. When he heard about the spot on his lungs he quit his 5 pack a day smoking habit cold turkey that same day! The doctors couldn't say for sure what it was unless they did a biopsy. Duco refused the biopsy and any treatment. He went back to a doctor when he started throwing up blood. He went back for another examination and found out that the spot on his lung was nothing but he now has cancer of the pancreas and he won't survive its attack. His health is sliding very fast.

I sat and talked to Mabel for a while. As she was talking I could only stare at her and picture her as a gang moll during the 1930's. I don't think I heard a word she said. I just couldn't look at her the same. I had to leave. I had a grave to go to and pay respects. I told Mable I'd be back and said I had a lot to do that day. I got up a said good buy, and left. I couldn't hug Mable hello or good buy anymore. It was hard seeing Duco like that. It was October and the doctor seemed to think he'll live for another 5 months. I doubted it. There wasn't enough left of him to make it that far.

I drove over to Grandpa Clyde's house next. He was home and mighty glad to see me. Clyde had a major stroke in the mid 50's. It left his left side paralyzed and he was speechless.

By now he had gained back most of his left side motor skill and most of his speech. He was able to drive a car, but I wouldn't want to be around him when he was driving. Finally in 1975 the police came to his house and took his license.

I asked him if he would like to guide me to Grandma Irene's grave. He said he would. We got into my car and went to the cemetery. He knew exactly where it was. It was a special moment for both of us. We just stood there for a while and looked at the grave stone. Between seeing Duco earlier and the shape he was in and then seeing my favorite person on earth buried below my feet and gone forever.

I broke down and cried. Grandpa looked at me and was confused; he couldn't understand how a big soldier like me could cry.

I only had one thing to say, "Hubert Humphrey said once, "A man without a tear is a man without a heart." Grandpa had a tear roll down his cheek.

I took Grandpa Clyde back home and stayed with him for a few hours. It was a nice talk; we caught up on the good old days. He had some of the most interesting stories. He was brought up in Iowa on a small farm. The guy hated snakes. He just shivered when he saw them. One day while driving his car down a dirt road he saw a huge black snake crossing the road. He aimed for it and he ran it over. He looked in his mirror and there was no dead snake in the road. He stopped the car and backed up. He wouldn't get out of the car or roll down the windows, but he still searched for that snake. He drove in circles looking for that darn critter. He finally assumed it was wrapped under the car waiting for him to step out.

He headed to the local creek crossing. He would wash the snake from under his car. He drove up and down the creek for about 15 minutes. He figured the snake was drowned and dead by now. He went home. When he got into the driveway, he honked the car horn. His dad came running out and asked what's wrong. Clyde told him about his ordeal and he was afraid to get out of the car. His dad kneeled down and crawled under the car. A second latter he crawled out holding a 4 foot long live corn snake! Clyde wouldn't come out of that car for another half hour. He was so afraid of snakes he would turn the channel on the TV if the show had a snake.

My day was complete. I did what I wanted to do. It was a Thursday and the weather man promised a huge snow storm that night. I went home to hunker down during the storm. Sure enough, we got a lot of snow that night and all day Friday. When dad got home from work he was chilled to the bone. He worked out side all day. Friday night wasn't a structured meal night. Everyone would just grab leftovers. Dad and I had leftovers from previous meals, beer and brandy.

About 7:00pm it was dark outside. He said he had something to show me, get your coat on. We went out to the garage and there stood a trailer with a covered snowmobile on it. Wow, I've never seen one of these. He said to help him get it off the trailer. We pulled it onto the snow on the driveway. He gave me instruction on how to run it and pulled the rope. Off I went. I drove all over the neighborhood for about 35 minuets; He flagged me back into the garage with it. When I got in he closed the door. It was still snowing hard. He said that the heavy snow will cover the tracks. Huh? He said it's illegal to drive then in city limits unless it's an emergency. We put it back on the trailer and said we would go up north tomorrow and ride around Mille Lacs. He had something up there to show me too. The rest of the evening we sat up drinking brandy and beer until we just feel asleep.

I would wake up in the arm chair now and then and notice dad snoring away. I thought he was very loud at that snoring. I'll bet mom is glad he out here for once. Then I fell to sleep for the rest of the night.

When I woke up I had a blanket on me and dad was in bed. Cheryl was walking around with a cup of coffee and sat in the room with me. We chatted for a while and caught up on her life. We talked until my other two sisters walked in and then we all just sat there and talked. We talked about everything, including Duco and Mable. We all had our thought about them. Cheryl was the favorite grandchild for Duco and Mable. Duco named his cruiser after her and bought her a car during her high school years. I don't blame Cheryl in any way, shape, or form for her insistence on declaring her grandparent victims of the times and should be forgotten and forgiven. They were her idols.

I disagree with her when it comes to their crimes and behavior being forgotten. We can't forget what these people did to other people. We need to learn by their mistakes. Forgiving them for their acts of violence and cruelty is up to the families and victims who they exploited. My own mother couldn't forgive Mable for what she did to her, how could I. I can't forget or forgive the things they did to me. What they did was to give me horrorable memories of my childhood. My other two sisters agree with me 100%. They were also victims of Mable's cruelty. Cheryl is a victim of their child abuses every bit as much as the rest of us. They abused her with kindness. They knew it would be a source irritation among the family when they would buy her a gift and nothing for the rest of us. Duco promised the girls if they got "A's in school, he would buy them all a car. They all got A's and Cheryl got the car.

A few years later when Mom and Mable decided to join the men up at the mobile home for a weekend. They all got fairly liquored up at Liberty Beach. At closing time they all went back to the trailer. Mom had a brave moment while they sat at the table for a night cap. She asked Mable again who her father was.

This is a very explosive subject when Mable was sober, now she' intoxicated and ready for this conversation. Mable was always ready for an argument. She just loved bringing out the "unwanted child" quote on her daughter. The argument was very heated and Mable being Mable wouldn't lighten up a bit. Arguing was her favorite pastime, she was a pro. My mother now getting nowhere with Mable made dad take her home immediately. Mable, Duco and mom wouldn't talk for months.

Their Final Chapter

Dad woke me early Saturday morning and told me to dress warm, we're going fishing. I got out every piece of cold weather clothing I had and put it on. I could barley move. We got in my car and he said, "Head for Mille Lac." We did. In a blizzard! It took 4 hours to get there but we made it. We went out of Eastside Resort. I thought he pre-rented a house and knew where it was. He guided me to a real nice looking fish house; it had his name on it. It was pink with fish cartoons painted on it. Inside there were bunk beds at the end, a heating stove and a cooking stove. It had battery operated lights, card table with four padded chairs, radio and color TV. Heck, Dad built a luxury house! We had a blast that week end and we caught fish.

It was mid February and the law stated the fish houses have to be off the ice by the end of the month. Also in mid February the Walleye season was finished until May. We went into the bar to have a beer. While in there the owner said we had a call from home and we needed to return the call. Dad called mom. When he came back he told me Duco had just died and they wanted us back there ASAP. We slammed our beer down and took off to the fish house. It was

Saturday, a day earlier than we planned to wrap things up. We tied down everything in the house to have it ready for the resort truck to pull it to shore for summer storage.

It took about three hours to drive in another snow storm to get to Mable's house. When we got there the first thing they wanted us to do was to make sure he was dead. I said, "Have you called the police or funeral home yet?" I looked at Duke with his eyes fixed on the ceiling and his tongue hanging out and he wasn't breathing, I said, "He's really dead. Call the funeral home." I've seen dead people. He's dead. I went out in the hallway and whispered in Dads ear, "I wonder if she killed him?" He chuckled, then looked at me and scowled. A few days later we buried Duco. It was February, 1970. Mabel was on her own and Duco didn't leave anything.

A couple years later Mom and I took over Mable's power of attorney. Mable had been stonewalled everywhere she looked for any accounts Duco may have left behind. The power of attorney gave us the authority to look at banks to determine if Duco left any money. We were not stonewalled. I think Mable imposed her bad attitude when talking to bankers. They didn't like it. We searched Minneapolis and St. Paul banks as well as several banks along Mille Lacs. Everyone figured Duco had money buried someplace. We even took the Caddy apart.

We took off the tires and had them remounted just so we could check inside them. Dad and I used the mobile home for one summer season. We found no treasure buried in the yard or in the banks.

Before we had power of attorney Mable received the balloon payment for the house on Portland. It was plenty of money and if invested right, she could have lived happily ever after. It didn't happen that way though. She gave away most of it to Mavis and took the rest to Las Vegas and spent it all. Eventually she couldn't pay the rent where she was. Mom and I set her up in a senior high rise with assisted living. While in there she wanted all of Duco's property at the lake auctioned off. Well, we did that and she got just pennies on the dollars for his tools. It was a giveaway.

Next she sold the lot and trailer. It was valued at $45,000 in 1975 dollars. She sold it for $10,000. The 5 year old Caddy went for $1500. Mabel lost over $40,000. She gave it to Mavis to open a ceramic shop. The rest went to a cousin who shall remain un-named. Mable was broke. She was back to her 1930's. This time Mom and I were stuck with her. I really think Mable was under the impression that she would live out her life at mom and dad's house or mine. I wasn't going to let that happen. We now had power of attorney on her, and I had a plan. I needed to check on her quality of life. First I asked the nurses and management how she was doing. They all stated that she was leaving food burn on the stove several times a week setting off the fire alarms and she was constantly pulling the chain in the bathroom for help getting up. She was leaving the tub water running and it was a problem once a week. She would get lost outside and they would have to gather up a search party to find her. They all agreed that she needs to see a doctor and get orders for total assisted living, a nursing home. I set it up for the following week. My plan was falling into place.

A few days later we got her to her doctor. We told him everything that was going on at the apartment and he thought she really needs to be under constant supervision, a nursing home. Of coarse Mable didn't agree with him because she thought she was going to live with her daughter. That was her wrong assumption. She burned that bridge years ago. It's off to a home for Mable. He wrote up a diagnosis and order. He also gave us a recommendation to Eagle Nursing Home in Bloomington, Minnesota. We got her back to her high rise and told her she would be moving next weekend and to get ready. We would send the girls to help her pack. Mom and I went to Eagle and just by luck they had an opening. They said Saturday would be fine.

That Friday we had a farewell party for her in her apartment. The family was there plus a neighbor or two. It was hastily put together. We all brought a small gift. When she picked ours up (I was married with one boy) she wound up tossed it at us and said, "I don't ever want anything from you Halverson's again!" That did it. We walked out.

Saturday morning I couldn't wait to get there. That old hag was going to ride with me the 30 miles to the nursing home. I wanted the tension so close you could cut it with a knife. That's exactly what happened too. She rode with me and kept her nose on the side widow all the way there. Once we got there the nursing staff was waiting for her on the sidewalk all lined up nice and neat in their uniforms. One of them had a wheel chair waiting at the curb. I stopped right next to the wheel chair. Mable got out kicking and screaming. She didn't want to be in a nursing home. Well, damn it! This is you home, deal with it! We got her to her room.

For almost two solid weeks she would call mom and beg to get her out of there. Mother finally had Mable's phone removed. Mable went through several room mates. She didn't know how to make friends. They put a deaf woman in there for a while, but then Mable would leave lights on all night. They finally put someone in there that actually listened to Mable's ramblings. It turned out to be spy from the home. They used her ramblings against her to modify her behavior. It worked.

Mable and I still had that "Hate you" attitude with each other. She still wouldn't tell mom who her real dad was. One day I brought Mable her favorite snack of beer and sardines. This usually put a smile on her face. This usually gave her gas. She gassed her roommate out of the room. As she wolfed down the snack, I nicely asked her why she wouldn't tell mom her real dads' name. She looked at me with her little beady eyes and said, "I hate you. I know people that will take care of you and nobody will ever find your body". I thought, "Hum, don't you think your friends are dead?" What a thing to say to your grandson. I said to her, "Grandma, I know how much you like it here. I hope you live a long time." I left.

Well, she did live a long time in that home. She made it until June, 1991. Dad had to pay for the funeral. It wasn't elaborate, that's for sure. We picked a casket a step up from cardboard, paid the fee for embalming and dressing her corpse. The church was free plus some church volunteers brought the food. Some people at her funeral thought the casket was cheap. Yes, it was cheap. The only reason she got a casket in the first place because she didn't want to be cremated.

If Mable would have set aside some of the money she gave away to the people that are now complaining she would have had a very nice casket. As it is, none of those whiners ever came up with a dime to help in the funeral cost, yet they had the biggest mouths saying it was cheap. I'm here to tell you, if I had my choice, it would have been a cardboard box and a pauper's grave. That would have been more than she deserved.

My time with Mable was done on that June day in 1991. I was relieved. Every time I saw that woman my stomach would growl. I never liked her. I have no forgiveness for that woman. I was a small kid and couldn't defend myself against her. That's when I first became another victim. When I stayed at their house overnight for one reason or another, I got real acquainted with her bedroom closet. It was there that she would lock me up for hours for infractions that I'm sure a little boy deserved. I really appreciated the opportunity to do all there lawn work as a 5 year old. Pickup twigs, mow the yard, sweep the sidewalk, sweep the garage, and clean the basement. If I had some time left over, go upstairs and clean the attic rooms. Yah, I really enjoyed going to their house. When Duco got home he would always inspect the daily chores. If they weren't done right, we would have to do it over again, and again and again. These people just never lightened up on us when we were kids. Duco would find ways to humiliate us one way or another.

One Thanksgiving Duco called me to where he was sitting. I went to him. He had a cigar sized box in his hand and said, "Here is some candy for you". He handed me the box. I grabbed the box and down I went. He had it rigged so it would deliver a huge electrical shock. It knocked me down and burned my fingers. He belly laughed over that until tears came out his eyes. Nobody else thought it was funny though. It hurt me bad. He had so much power in that box it could have stopped my heart. He looked around and noticed nobody laughing so he put the box away. I never saw that box again. Thing is, he made his point. He had the power to hurt someone if he wanted.

Cleon would often visit everyone and the Thanksgiving Day dinner. As far as the rest of the gang goes I don't know where Walter, Blanch, or Margaret disappeared too. After their release from prison they ran away like released caged animals never to be heard from again. Nobody, and I mean nobody ever heard or seen them again.

Cleon remarried for a short period of time and had two children, then divorced again. After this marriage he reverted back to his underworld cronies. He hung around exotic dancer clubs for gentlemen. I said it before and now I'll repeat it. The guy had charm oozing out all over him.

He was a Minneapolis Clark Cable look alike, even sporting the moustache. He was a fancy dresser, usually in a suit and tie. He always had a beautiful dancer on his arm everywhere he went.

When he visited us at the river lot, he would always have one of these exotic girls with him. They would either wink at me or give me a kiss on the cheek. Candy Kane was his favorite. Mine too. I was 11-12 years old and I would nearly pass out from their attention. I think Cleon put them up to it. I liked Cleon, especially his girlfriends.

One night Cleon was coming back from Montevideo. It was very late at night and he fell asleep at the wheel doing 75 miles per hour. The car found the biggest Oak tree off the road near Excelsior. Cleon lived, but he was in a body cast for over a half a year. When he finally got out of the cast the first thing he did was hit the strip clubs. One night he and his buddy wanted to move to another bar for a poker game. His drunken friend was driving through Minneapolis better than 90 miles per hour. About a block ahead of them a tractor with trailer pulled out in front of them. They couldn't stop. They went under the trailer and both were decapitated. That was the end of Cleon.

Surviving Relatives

The first book generated a lot of phone calls to my publisher with people wanting to meet me. They were relatives and people that were around during the capture in 1933. I was overwhelmed with their fascination with the book. I met up with some of these people in Willmar, Minnesota in mid May, 2007. One of the persons I met was Elsie. She is a fascinating woman. She was my mothers' playmate when mother stayed in Montevideo. She is also a distant cousin and the family historian. That day she brought some very interesting papers and pamphlets all relating to the family history. The only thing she had about the gang was an old detective magazine with an inflated story of the gang's capture. The Bonrud's never did get a complete true story about the gang and the magazine didn't help. It was a 1933 version of our modern day tabloids. They are the magazines that tell you what you want to hear and not what really happened.

I don't believe that particular detective magazine is in business anymore, but the careless writing of their story with all the guessing and dramatizing certainly hurt a nice family. I wrote the Bonrud

Gang story based on fact. It was from historical documents and one on one interview with people that had direct knowledge of the incidents. I still compile information from reliable sources today. For instance, one family member mentions that when they came to town they were known as the "Snatchers". Not just for their ability to snatch people, the gang started out as chicken thieves! They were snatching chickens from various farmers for their evening meal. The magazine picked up on that title and called the story, "The capture of the Snatchers". It's also written in the magazine that the Minneapolis Police originally tagged them the Snatchers and after the capture they became known as the Bonrud Gang.

Another part of the magazine I find most interesting is a picture of Noble lying on the morgues table. It is a head shot showing his neck wound. The caption said, "This picture of the leader was taken while he drew his last breath." What is he doing in the morgue if he was still breathing? I would think he would be in the hospital. The coroner's inquest stated he died before he hit the ground. Oscar frisked his dead body where it fell.

Noble was not the leader of the gang. There was no real leader; it was run by mutual agreement. If anyone would have been the leader it would have been Cleon. He was the smartest one in the group. The story of the Bonrud Gang was national interest. It's no wonder. They had shootouts with police on at least three occasions.

They confessed to over 63 major felonies committed in three states. There were four men with three good looking women at their side. All of them had the same criminal ambitions. I wonder, did they confess to all the crimes they committed? I highly doubt it.

I have been questioned as to why I would write about the dark side of my family. The answer is as complicated as the gang is. I made a promise to my mother. She wanted her parents exposed for who they really were. My grandparents put on a façade of being a sweet old couple. This is far from the truth but they were professional manipulators. They had a lot of people fooled.

I was brought up during a time when little boys are to be seen and not heard. Speaking up could be painful. Grandparents had more power over their families. Special circumstances allowed my grandparents to have too much power over my family. Alcohol was a major factor in the way we kids were treated back then. There was no 911 and there was no place for an abused child to run. It became a matter of endurance.

During the 1920's and 1930's child abuse was unspoken. It was considered normal to whack the kids around and work them as child labor. Sexual deviants weren't talked about. They weren't treated as criminals. They were shoved off to the side and allowed to continue their activity out of sight and minds of authority. I challenge readers to look at newspaper archives and locate any story of sexual misbehavior committed by adults upon children. Show me a newspaper article that exposed a pedophile and an arrest and trial. I couldn't find one.

This ignorance carried on for many years. As I grew up in Bloomington a pedophile lived across the street from us. For identification we will call him Mr. K. He lived alone and always had his shades drawn. One day my friend and I were walking up the street. This person poked his head out the door and asked my friend to come in his house. He had something to show him. My friend was curious and fell for the trap. As he walked in the house Mr. K. told me to go home.

An hour later my friend called me from his house and told me to come over he had to talk to me. He just lived two doors down and it took me a minute to get there. His parents weren't home and he was sitting at the kitchen table sipping on a ketchup bottle.

He then told me of the sickest sexual acts I ever heard of to that day. I listened to him for over an hour. He wanted to take a bath and go to bed so I went back home.

I couldn't hold that news in me. I told my mother about it. She was just about in tears thinking how horrible that must have been. Then she thought it could have been me. She called my friend and asked him if she could do anything for him. He said no and he just wanted to lie down.

That's as far as it went. I believe he molested little boys until he died from a heart attack a few months later.

Today we don't let kids out of our sight. We are under the impression that a pedophile lives under every rock we see. If a child is molested today, the molester will wish he/she was never born when our courts get hold of them. Even prisoners can't live with child molesters. They use a bit of street justice on them in prison.

Gangs are another problem. There is still a Mafia out there. They are stealthy and very well organized. Groups like the Hell's Angels are also still around. Drug cartels can be classified as gangs and so can those Nazi extremist claiming white power be called gangs. There are all sorts of gangs in our country. I guess the ones we are all familiar with are the young punks that roam the streets at night looking for anyone that has imposed on their territory. Then when a violator is found, they simply shoot them on the spot. These gangsters are kids. They are hardly old enough to grow a whisker. What made them powerful are the guns they carried and the attitude they are taught by their peers and parents.

Let me just say this to these little boys and girls. "Until you pay taxes and a mortgage you have no territory. I pay taxes. You are operating in my territory. Get out! Go to school. Get a job. Volunteer in an organization that helps people. Just so you know, I enforce my territory with a police department. They have guns too.

Acknowledgements

The first book, "If Grandma's in Heaven, Watch out! The 1930's Bonrud Gang" was a bit nerve racking because I exposed my family to the public. Then I thought what the heck, it's the bad side of the family I wanted exposed and they have been in the public eye before.

It's the law enforcement officials that have for generations fascinated me the most. Their memories were as sharp as a tack. Each county has a historical document of one kind or another for the public to review. I went and searched every one of them. I talked with people on the street and asked them if they remembered the Bonrud Gang. Quit a few did and they had a story to tell about them. My thanks go to all the people that shared their time with me to discuss the past.

The first book also brought out my blood relatives who were itching to meet me. They stated the book set them free of the bondage of shame they have endured over the years. Back then the bandits shamed the rest of the family and the general population would shun the Bonrud's. They lost jobs, couldn't use public rest rooms, or attend the church of their choice. This is sad but true.

The book with all the facts is slowly healing those wounds. The facts of the matter have come to light and now the neighbors can understand that there were just a few bad ones in the Bonrud family, and the good ones in the family weren't any less disgusted with them.

I have found relatives I never knew I had. Thanks to Elsie who I met in Willmar in late May, 2007. She is the official family historian. She swamped me with interesting information. She told me stories that just made me shake my head. Another cousin is Waunita. She was a delight to meet. To all the people that I have been in contact with from the Montevideo area, thank you all for you input. You are the family I never knew and now the family I'll never forget.

This book reveals more on the life after prison. They were just as cruel and abusive after prison. The fights they had together were always hot and heated and nearly resulted in murder. I was there! I heard these fights and saw the fighting that resulted from an argument. They were scary. I can only imagine how there victims must have seen them during the crime.

The madness in their eyes would have been scary enough. I've seen that look in Mable's eyes the day she threatened my life. Even at 80 plus years old and in the nursing home I irritated her with a question about my real grandfather. I just wanted some generic information about him. She knew who he was but for reasons unknown, she never would give us his name. That day I pressed a bit harder. Her comment was, "I know people that would take care of you and nobody would ever find your body". What a sweet old lady.

Threaten your grandson with murder. I knew she had nobody that would perform such an act, but the look in her eyes transformed her into a murderous look that will never be forgotten. I wondered, when she was young, how many times did she exposed that look to her victims.

All the information in this book has been taken from police reports, court records, Minnesota Department of Corrections, Minnesota Historical Society, Chippewa County Historical Society, Swift County Historical Society, personal interviews with people that had knowledge of the events that took place in 1933 and my own personal experiences with the characters mentioned in the book.

Facts are written as stated from various reports and some opinions are based on my interpretation of the circumstances and facts. Some names have been changed to protect their privacy.

I need to thank my best friend Marty. He has been with me for many years always doing what best friends do best, be there for me when I need him. We worked together until our retirements. Marty was a police officer and I was a Park Ranger. He can read me like a book and always finds the words to make life better for me. A person once told me that best friends can sometimes spend time together and not say a word. We are best friends.

My new found friend Gerald from Maynard, Minnesota can only be described as my long distant friend that knows what it takes to make his friends feel at home. This is a friendship that I hope will last forever like the one with I have with Marty.

Both of these fine gentlemen have inspired me to keep writing and enjoy life. I'm a better person knowing both of them. Their friendship is worth more than gold to me. this computer. My wife Marsha has been most patient with me during this writing. Also in between some of this writing I have made several trips to the hospital addressing my heart issues.

At this writing I have 16 stents in by hearts arteries plus a pacemaker. Writing this book had nothing to do with the heart condition, it's totally generic. I only mention it to explain how devoted I am to telling this story. I believe there are thousands of children out there that live in fear of a parent or relative. If you are the abuser, stop. Look at yourself for once and stare deep into your soul. You have to stop and get help. To my readers, pay attention to your family and friends. If you suspect abuse, intervene by calling authorities. Just do it.

Photos

This is the new 1933 Buick. It's a wonder nobody was hit by bullets. There were a total of nine holes in the car. It begs the question, how many bullets did the gang fire at Oscar? The shootout must have been spectacular.

On the left are pictured Duco, Walter and Cleon in front of the Chippewa County Jail. Not shown are the armed police officers standing by with guns drawn. Look closely and you will notice these men are chained together. Duco exposes a chain around his waist and the other two have glints of hand cuffs. On the right is the Bonrud farm in 1942. It was taken from on top of the barn.

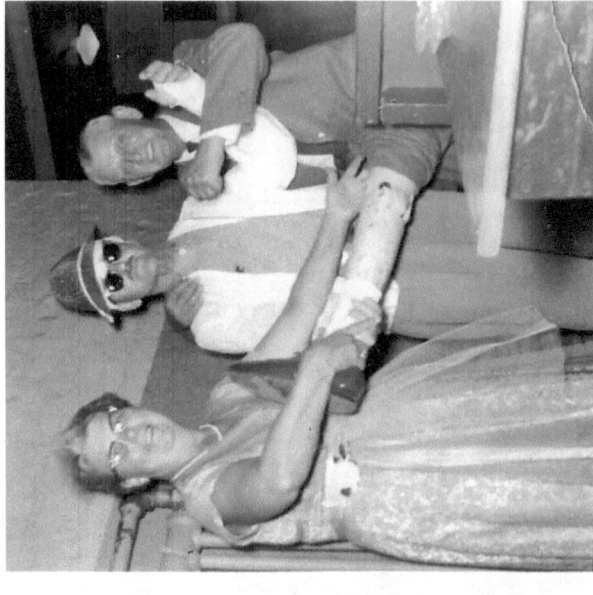

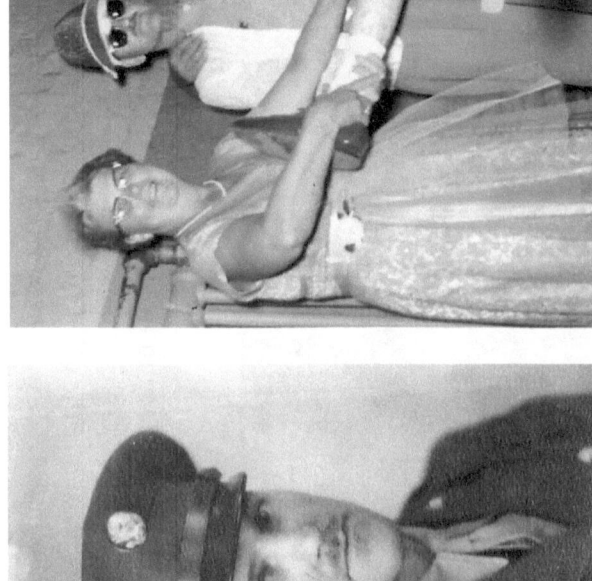

(Left) Cleon was released from prison with the promise to enlist in the Army.

(Right) Cleon fell to sleep at the wheel near Excelsior, Minnesota on Highway 7. He ran into the largest tree along the stretch of road and this is the result. Shortly

After the body cast and head gear was removed, he went riding with a friend in Minneapolis. The car ran under a semi trailer at 65 MPH. Both were decapitated. Pictured is his sister, Elva and her husband Art. Art's legs were shot of at the Armory while setting up targets for machine gunners. One soldier fired too soon.

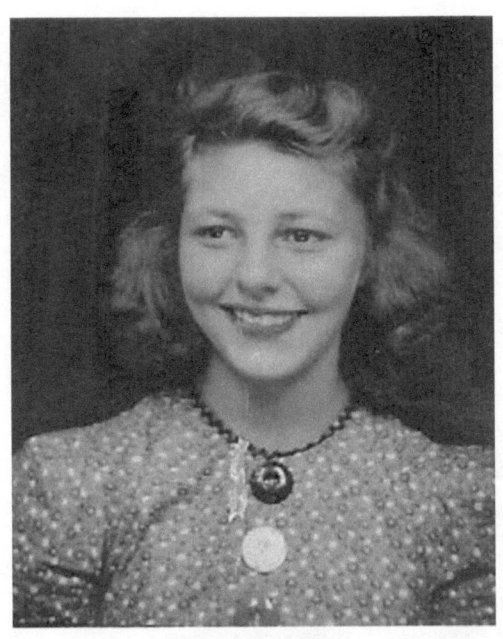

(Top) Pictured is my mother, Darlos, as a teenager. She was living at home with Duco and Mable.

(Bottom) My dad would visit my mother every day at the nursing home. This would be her last Christmas. Stricken with complications from diabetes she would pass away June 30, 2004. She was 77 years old.

This is Duco doing what he did best.
The gangster attitude was always there. This was taken in 1948. He
was totally released from his sentence.

Mable holding me in 1949.

About the Author

After my first book, "If Grandma's In Heaven, Watch Out! The 1930's Bonrud Gang", people asked me what ever happened to my grandparents. They went to prison, of coarse, and they just weren't very good citizens after their release. I grew up with them and I was never comfortable around them. Grandma and grandpa were very abusive and controlling. I knew what my mother went through as a child and I wrote about her experiences. Now I wanted to put my experiences in writing in case anyone thought for a second the first book was exaggerated in any way.

The truth is stranger than fiction and I lived the truth. I spent many hours debating if I should write about my family like this but, hopefully they will see my point of view and the true hardships I faced growing up and have a better understanding on how I became the person I am today.

I'm 61 years old and I remember most of these circumstances as if they happened yesterday. There are just some things a person can't forget.

Just maybe some person will read this true story and see the things I have seen. Maybe they will see the same thing inside themself or with someone else and do something to stop it. If that were to happen, my life is fulfilled.